A STUDY IN
TERROR

ELLERY QUEEN
A STUDY IN
TERROR

Xanadu

British Cataloguing in Publication Data

Queen, Ellery
  A study in terror. – (The Great detective series)
  I. Title
  813.52
  ISBN 1-85480-052-3

Copyright © Ellery Queen 1966

First published in the USA 1966

This edition published 1991 by Xanadu Publications Limited
19 Cornwall Road, London N4 4PH

Printed and bound in Great Britain by
Cox & Wyman, Reading

Ellery Begins

ELLERY BROODED

For a reasonable time.

After which he got up from his typewriter, seized ten pages of doomed copy, and tore them into four ragged sections.

He scowled at the silent typewriter. The machine leered back.

The phone rang, and he jumped for it as if it were a life-preserver.

"Don't snarl at *me*," said a hurt voice with undertones of anguish. "I'm having fun, per orders."

"Dad! Did I snap at you? I'm in a plot bind. How's Bermuda?"

"Sunshine, blue water, and more damn sand than you can shake a billy at. I want to come *home*."

"No," Ellery said firmly. "The trip cost me a bundle, and I'm going to get my money's worth."

Inspector Queen's sigh was eloquent. "You always were a dictator where I'm concerned. What am I, a basket case?"

"You're overworked."

"Maybe I could arrange a rebate?" Inspector Queen suggested hopefully.

"Your orders are to rest and relax—forget everything."

"Okay, okay. There's a hot horseshoe game going on across from my cabana. Maybe I can horn in."

"Do that, dad. I'll phone tomorrow for the score."

Ellery hung up and glared at the typewriter. The problem remained. He circled the table warily and began to pace.

Providentially, the doorbell rang.

"Leave them on the table," Ellery called. "Take the money."

The visitor disobeyed. Feet crossed the foyer and entered the scene of the great man's agony. Ellery grunted. "You? I thought it was the boy with the delicatessen."

Grant Ames, III, with the aplomb of the privileged bore —a bore with millions—aimed his perfect Brooks Brothers towards the bar. There he exchanged the large manila envelope he was carrying for a bottle of scotch and a glass. "I came to make a delivery, too," Ames announced. "Something a hell of a lot more important than pastrami," and sat down on the sofa. "You stock pretty good scotch, Ellery."

"I'm glad you like it. Take the bottle with you. I'm working."

"But I claim the prerogative of a fan. I devour every one of your stories."

"Borrowed from unscrupulous friends," Ellery growled.

"That," Grant said, pouring, "is unkind. You'll apologize when you know my mission."

"What mission?"

"A delivery. Weren't you listening?"

"Of what?"

"That envelope. By the gin."

Ellery turned in that direction. Grant waved him back. "I insist on filling you in first, Maestro."

The doorbell rang again. This time it was the sandwiches. Ellery stamped into the foyer and returned with his mouth full.

"Why don't you go to work, Grant? Get a job in one of your father's frozen-food plants. Or become a pea-picker.

8

Anything, but get out of my hair. I've got work to do, I tell you."

"Don't change the subject," Grant III said. "You wouldn't have a kosher pickle there, would you? I'm crazy about kosher pickles."

Ellery offered him a slice of pickle and collapsed in his chair. "All right, damn it. Let's get it over with. Fill me in on what?"

"The background. Yesterday afternoon there was a do up in Westchester. I attended."

"A do," Ellery said, looking envious.

"Swimming. A little tennis. That sort of thing. Not many on the scene."

"Most people have the bad habit of working on week-day afternoons."

"You can't make me feel guilty with that kind of drivel," said the playboy. "I'm doing you a service. I acquired the envelope mysteriously, and I bring it to your door as instructed."

"As instructed by whom?" Ellery had still not glanced at the envelope.

"I haven't any idea. When I made my escape, I found it lying on the seat of my Jag. Someone had written on the envelope, 'Please deliver to Ellery Queen.' The way I figure it, it's someone who holds you in too much awe to make the personal approach. And who's aware of our deathless friendship."

"Sounds dreary. Look Grant, is this something you've made up? I'm damned if I'm going to play games with you at a time like this. I've got that demon deadline breathing down my neck. Go diddle around with one of your playgirls, will you?"

"The envelope." Grant came up like an athlete and went and got it and brought it back. "Here. Duly delivered. From hand to hand. Do with it what you will."

9

"What am I supposed to do with it?" asked Ellery sourly.

"No idea. It's a manuscript. Handwritten. Looks quite old. Read it, I suppose."

"Then you've examined it?"

"I felt it my duty. It may have been poison-pen stuff. Even pornography. Your sensibilities, old buddy. I had to consider them."

Ellery was studying the inscription with grudging curiosity. "Written by a woman."

"I found the contents quite harmless, however," Grant went on, nursing his glass. "Harmless, but remarkable."

"A standard envelope," Ellery muttered. "Sized to accommodate eight-and-a-half by eleven sheets."

"I swear, Ellery, you have the soul of a bookkeeper. Aren't you going to open it?"

Ellery undid the clasp and pulled out a cardboard-backed notebook with the word *Journal* printed on it in a large, old-fashioned script.

"Well," he said. "It does look old."

Grant regarded him with a sly smile as Ellery opened the ledger, or notebook, studied the first page with widening eyes, turned over, read, turned over again, read again.

"My God," he said. "This purports to be an adventure of Sherlock Holmes in the original manuscript, handwritten by Dr. Watson!"

"Would you say it's authentic?"

Ellery's silvery eyes glittered. "You've read it, you say?"

"I couldn't resist."

"Are you familiar with Watson's style?"

"I," Grant said, admiring the color of the scotch in his glass, "am an *aficionado*. Sherlock Holmes, Ellery Queen, Eddie Poe. Yes, I'd say it's authentic."

"You authenticate easily, my friend." Ellery glanced at his typewriter with a frown; it seemed far away.

"I thought you'd be excited."

"I would if this were on the level. But an unknown Holmes story!" He riffled through the pages. "And what's more, from the look of it, a novel. A lost novel!" He shook his head.

"You don't believe it."

"I stopped believing in Santa Claus at the age of three, Grant. You, you were born with Santa Claus in your mouth."

"Then you think it's a forgery."

"I don't think anything yet. But the odds that it is are astronomical."

"Why would anyone go to all this trouble?"

"For the same reason people climb mountains. For the hell of it."

"The least you can do is read the first chapter."

"Grant, I don't have the time!"

"For a new Sherlock Holmes novel?" Back at the bar Ames poured himself another scotch. "I'll sit here quietly guzzling and wait." He went back to the sofa and crossed his long legs comfortably.

"Damn you." For a long moment Ellery glared at the notebook. Then he sighed, sounding remarkably like his father, and settled back and began to read.

From the Journal
of
John Watson, M.D.

CHAPTER I

THE SURGEON'S-KIT

"YOU ARE QUITE right, Watson. The Ripper may well be a woman."

It was a crisp morning in the autumn of the year 1888. I was no longer residing permanently at No. 221B, Baker Street. Having married, and thus become weighted with the responsibility of providing for a wife—a most delightful responsibility—I had gone into practice. Thus, the intimate relationship with my friend Mr. Sherlock Holmes had dwindled to occasional encounters.

On Holmes's side, these consisted of what he mistakenly termed "impositions upon your hospitality," when he required my services as an assistant or a confidant. "You have such a patient ear, my dear fellow," he would say, a preamble which always brought me pleasure, because it meant that I might again be privileged to share in the danger and excitement of another chase. Thus, the thread of my friendship with the great detective remained intact.

My wife, the most understanding of women, accepted this situation like Griselda. Those who have been so constant to my inadequate accounts of Mr. Sherlock Holmes's cases of detection will remember her as Mary Morstan, whom I providentially met while I was involved, with Holmes, in the case I have entitled *The Sign of Four*. As devoted a wife as any man could boast, she had patiently left me to my own devices on too many long evenings, whilst I perused my notes on Holmes's old cases.

One morning at breakfast, Mary said, "This letter is from Aunt Agatha."

I laid down my newspaper. "From Cornwall?"

"Yes, the poor dear. Spinsterhood has made her life a lonely one. Now her doctor has ordered her to bed."

"Nothing serious, I trust."

"She gave no such indication. But she is in her late seventies, and one never knows."

"Is she completely alone?"

"No. She has Beth, my old nanny, with her, and a man to tend the premises."

"A visit from her favourite niece would certainly do her more good than all the medicine in the world."

"The letter does include an invitation—a plea, really— but I hesitated..."

"I think you should go, Mary. A fortnight in Cornwall would benefit you also. You have been a little pale lately."

This statement of mine was entirely sincere; but another thought, a far darker one, coloured it. I ventured to say that, upon that morning in 1888, every responsible man in London would have sent his wife, or sister, or sweetheart, away, had the opportunity presented itself. This, for a single, all-encompassing reason. Jack the Ripper prowled the night-streets and dark alleys of the city.

Although our quiet home in Paddington was distant in many ways from the Whitechapel haunts of the maniac, who could be certain? Logic went by the boards where the dreadful monster was concerned.

Mary was thoughtfully folding the envelope. "I don't like to leave you here alone, John."

"I assure you I'll be quite all right."

"But a change would do you good, too, and there seems to be a lull in your practice."

"Are you suggesting that I accompany you?"

Mary laughed. "Good heavens, no! Cornwall would bore you to tears. Rather that you pack a bag and visit your friend Sherlock Holmes. You have a standing invitation at Baker Street, as well I know."

I am afraid my objections were feeble. Her suggestion was a most alluring one. So, with Mary off to Cornwall and arrangements relative to my practice quickly made, the transition was achieved; to Holmes's satisfaction, I flatter myself in saying, as well as to my own.

It was surprising how easily we fell into the well-remembered routine. Even though I knew I could never again be satisfied with the old life, my renewed proximity to Holmes was delightful. Which brings me, in somewhat circuitous fashion, back to Holmes's remark out of the blue. He went on, "The possibility of a female monster cannot by any means be ignored."

It was the same old cryptic business, and I must confess that I was slightly annoyed. "Holmes! In the name of all that's holy, I gave no indication whatever that such a thought was passing through my mind."

Holmes smiled, enjoying the game. "Ah, but confess, Watson. It was."

"Very well. But—"

"And you are quite wrong in saying that you gave no indication of your trend of thought."

"But I was sitting here quietly—motionless, in fact!—reading my *Times*."

"Your eyes and your head were far from motionless, Watson. As you read, your eyes were trained on the extreme left-hand column of the newspaper, that which contains an account of Jack the Ripper's latest atrocity. After a time, you turned your gaze away from the story, frowning in anger. The thought that such a monster should be able to roam London's streets with impunity was clearly evident."

"That is quite true."

"Then, my dear fellow, your eyes, seeking a resting-place, fell upon that copy of the *Strand Magazine* lying beside your chair. It happens to be open to an advertisement in which Beldell's is offering ladies' evening gowns at what they purport to be a bargain-price. One of the gowns in the advertisement is displayed upon a model. Instantly, your expression changed; it became reflective. An idea had dawned upon you. The expression persisted as you raised your head and re-directed your gaze towards the portrait of her Majesty which hangs beside the fireplace. After a moment, your expression cleared, and you nodded to yourself. You had become satisfied with the idea that had come to you. At which point, I agreed. The Ripper could well be a female."

"But Holmes—"

"Come, now, Watson. Your retirement from the lists has dulled your perceptions."

"But when I glanced at the *Strand* advertisement, I could have had any of a dozen thoughts!"

"I disagree. Your mind was totally occupied with the story of the Ripper, and surely the advertisement concerning ladies' evening gowns was too far afield from your ordinary interests to divert your thoughts. Therefore, the idea that came to you had to be adjunct to your ponderings upon the monster. You verified this by raising your eyes to the Queen's portrait upon the wall."

"May I ask how that indicated my thought?" asked I, tartly.

"Watson! You certainly saw neither the model nor our gracious Queen as suspects. Therefore, you were scrutinising them as women."

"Granted," I retorted, "but would I not have been more likely to regard them as victims?"

"In that case, your expression would have reflected com-

15

passion, rather than that of a bloodhound come suddenly upon the scent."

I was forced to confess defeat. "Holmes, again you destroy yourself by your own volubility."

Holmes's heavy brows drew together. "I do not follow."

"Imagine what an image you would create were you to refuse all explanations of your amazing deductions!"

"But at what expense," said he, drily, "to your melodramatic accounts of my trifling adventures."

I threw up my hands in surrender; and Holmes, who rarely indulged in more than a smile, on this occasion echoed my hearty laughter.

"So long as the subject of Jack the Ripper has arisen," said I, "allow me a further question. Why have you not interested yourself in the grisly affair, Holmes? If for no other reason, it would be a signal service to London."

Holmes's long, thin fingers made an impatient gesture. "I have been busy. As you know, I returned from the Continent only recently, where the mayor of a certain city retained me to solve a most curious riddle. Knowing your turn of mind, I presume you would call it *The Case of the Legless Cyclist*. One day I shall give you the details for your files."

"I shall be delighted to get them! But you *are* back in London, Holmes, and this monster is terrorising the city. I should think you would feel obligated—"

Holmes scowled. "I am obligated to no one."

"Pray do not misunderstand me—"

"I'm sorry, my dear Watson, but you should know me well enough to assume my total indifference towards such a case."

"At the risk of appearing more dense than most of my neighbours—"

"Consider! When given a choice, have I not always sought out problems of an intellectual character? Have

I not always been drawn to adversaries of stature? Jack the Ripper, indeed! What possible challenge could this demented oaf present? A slavering cretin roaming the streets after dark, striking at random."

"He has baffled the London Police."

"I venture to suggest that that may reflect the short-comings of Scotland Yard rather than any particular cleverness on the part of the Ripper."

"But still—"

"The thing will end soon enough. I daresay that one of these nights Lestrade will trip over the Ripper while the maniac is in the process of committing a murder, and thus bring him triumphantly to book."

Holmes was chronically annoyed with Scotland Yard for not measuring up to his own stern efficiency; for all his genius, he could be childishly obstinate on such occasions. But further comment from me was cut off by the ringing of the downstairs bell. There was a slight delay; then we heard Mrs. Hudson ascending, and it was with astonishment that I observed her entrance. She was carrying a brown paper parcel and a pail of water, and she wore an expression of sheer fright.

Holmes burst out laughing for the second time that morning. "It's quite all right, Mrs. Hudson. The package appears harmless enough. I'm sure we shall not need the water."

Mrs. Hudson breathed a sigh of relief. "If you say so, Mr. Holmes. But since that last experience, I was taking no chances."

"And your alertness is to be commended," said Holmes, as he took the parcel. After his long-suffering landlady left, he added, "Just recently, Mrs. Hudson brought me a parcel. It was in connection with an unpleasant little affair I brought to a satisfactory conclusion, and it was sent by a vengeful gentleman who under-estimated the keenness of

17

my hearing. The ticking of the mechanism was quite audible to me, and I called for a pail of water. The incident gave Mrs. Hudson a turn from which she has still not recovered."

"I don't wonder!"

"But what have we here? Hmmm. Approximately fifteen inches by six. Four inches thick. Neatly wrapped in ordinary brown paper. Post-mark, Whitechapel. The name and address written by a woman, I should hazard, who seldom puts pen to paper."

"That seems quite likely, from the clumsy scrawl. And that is certainly done in a woman's hand."

"Then we agree, Watson. Excellent! Shall we delve deeper?"

"By all means!"

The arrival of the parcel had aroused his interest, not to mention mine; his deep-set grey eyes grew bright when he removed the wrappings and drew forth a flat leather case. He held it up for my inspection. "Well, now. What do you make of this, Watson?"

"It is a surgeon's instrument-case."

"And who would be better qualified to know? Would you not say also that it is expensive?"

"Yes. The leather is of superb quality. And the workmanship is exquisite."

Holmes set the case upon the table. He opened it, and we fell silent. It was a standard set of instruments, each fitting snugly into its appropriate niche in the crimson-velvet lining of the case. One niche was empty.

"Which instrument is missing, Watson?"

"The large scalpel."

"The post-mortem knife," said Holmes, nodding and whipping out his lens. "And now, what does this case tell us?" As he examined the case and its contents closely, he went on. "To begin with the obvious, these instruments

18

belonged to a medical man who came upon hard times."

Obliged, as usual, to confess my blindness, I said, "I am afraid that is more obvious to you than to me."

Preoccupied with his inspection, Holmes replied absently, "If you should fall victim to misfortune, Watson, which would be the last of your possessions to reach the pawnbroker's shop?"

"My medical instruments, of course. But—"

"Precisely."

"Wherein do you perceive that this case was pledged?"

"There is double proof. Observe, just there, through my lens."

I peered at the spot he indicated. "A white smudge."

"Silver-polish. No surgeon would cleanse his instruments with such a substance. These have been treated like common cutlery by someone concerned only with their appearance."

"Now that you point it out, Holmes, I must agree. And what is your second proof?"

"These chalk-marks along the spine of the case. They are almost worn away, but if you will examine them closely, you will see that they constitute a number. Such a number as a pawnbroker would chalk upon a pledged article. Obviously, the counterpart of the number upon the pawn-ticket."

I felt the choler rising to my face. It was all too evident to me now.

"Then the kit was stolen!" I exclaimed. "Stolen from some surgeon, and disposed of, for a pittance, in a pawnshop!" My readers will forgive my indignation, I am sure; it was difficult for me to accept the alternative—that the practitioner would have parted with the instruments of a noble calling under even the most grievous circumstances.

Holmes, however, soon disillusioned me. "I fear, my dear Watson," said he, quite cheerfully, "that you do not perceive the finer aspects of the evidence. Pawn-brokers are a canny breed. It is part of their stock-in-trade not only to appraise the articles brought to them for pledge, but the persons offering them as well. Had the broker who dispensed his *largesse* for this surgical case entertained the slightest suspicion that it had been stolen, he would not have displayed it in his shop-window, as of course you observe he has done."

"As of course I do not!" said I, testily. "How can you possibly know that the case has been displayed in a window?"

"Look closely," said Holmes. "The case lay open in a place exposed to the sun; does not the faded velvet on the inner surface of the lid tell us that? Moreover, the pronounced character of the fading marks the time-span as an appreciable one. Surely this adds up to a shop-window?"

I could only nod. As always, when Holmes explained his astonishing observations, they appeared child's-play.

"It is a pity," said I, "that we do not know where the pawnshop lies. This curious gift might merit a visit to its source."

"Perhaps in good time, Watson," said Holmes, with a dry chuckle. "The pawnshop in question is well off the beaten track. It faces south, on a narrow street. The broker's business is not flourishing. Also, he is of foreign extraction. Surely you see that?"

"I see nothing of the sort!" said I, nettled again.

"To the contrary," said he, placing his finger-tips together and regarding me kindly, "you see everything, my dear Watson; what you fail to do is to observe. Let us take my conclusions in order. These instruments were not snatched up by any of the numerous medical students in the City of London, which would assuredly have been the case had the shop lain on a well-travelled thoroughfare. Hence my remark that it lies off the beaten track."

"But why must it face south on a narrow street?"

"Note the location of the bleached area. It runs neatly along the uppermost edge of the velvet lining, not elsewhere. Therefore, the sun touched the open case only at its zenith, when its rays were not obstructed by the buildings on the opposite side of the street. Thus the pawnshop stands on the north side of a narrow street."

"And your observation of the pawnbroker as of foreign extraction?"

"Observe the numeral *seven* in the chalked pledgemark on the spine. There is a short cross-mark on the ascender. Only a foreigner crosses his sevens in such a fashion."

I felt, as usual, like a fifth-form school-boy who had forgotten the words to the national anthem. "Holmes, Holmes," said I, shaking my head, "I shall never cease to marvel—"

But he was not listening. Again, he had stooped over the case, inserting his tweezers beneath the velvet lining. It gave way, and he peeled it off.

"Aha! What have we here? An attempt at concealment?"

"Concealment? Of what? Stains? Scratches?"

He pointed a long, thin finger. "That."

"Why, it's a coat of arms!"

"One with which I confess I am not familiar. Therefore, Watson, be kind enough to hand me down my copy of *Burke's Peerage*."

He continued to study the crest as I moved dutifully towards the bookshelves, murmuring to himself. "Stamped into the leather of the case. The surface is still in excellent condition." He came erect. "A clue to the character of the man who owned the case."

"He was careful with his possessions, perhaps?"

"Perhaps. But I was referring to—"

He broke off. I had handed him the Burke, and he leafed swiftly through the pages. "Ah, here we have it!" After a quick scrutiny, Holmes closed the book, laid it on the table, and dropped into a chair. He stared intently into space with his piercing eyes.

I could contain my patience no longer. "The crest, Holmes! Whose is it?"

"I beg your pardon, Watson," said Holmes, coming to with a start. "Shires. Kenneth Osbourne, the Duke of Shires."

The name was well-known to me, as indeed to all England. "An illustrious line."

Holmes nodded absently. "The estates, unless I mistake, lie in Devonshire, hard by the moors, among hunting-lands well regarded by noble sportsmen. The manor house—it is more of a feudal castle in appearance—is some four hundred years old, a classic example of Gothic architecture. I know little of the Shires's history, beyond the patent fact that the name has never been connected with the world of crime."

"So Holmes," said I, "we are back to the original question."

"Indeed we are."

"Which is: this surgeon's-case—why was it sent to you?"

"A provocative question."

"Perhaps an explanatory letter was delayed."

"You may well have hit upon the answer, Watson," said Holmes. "Therefore, I suggest we give the sender a little time, let us say until—" he paused to reach for his well-worn Bradshaw's, that admirable guide to British rail movements "—until ten-thirty to-morrow morning. If an explanation is not then forthcoming, we shall repair to Paddington Station and board the Devonshire express."

"For what reason, Holmes?"

"For two reasons. A short journey across the English countryside, with its changing colours at this time of year, should greatly refresh two stodgy Londoners."

"And the other?"

The austere face broke into the most curious smile. "In all justice," said my friend Holmes, "the Duke of Shires should have his property returned to him, should he not?" And he sprang to his feet and seized his violin.

"Wait, Holmes!" said I. "There is something in this you have not told me."

"No, no, my dear Watson," said he, drawing his bow briskly across the strings. "It is simply a feeling I have, that we are about to embark upon deep waters."

Ellery Continues

ELLERY RAISED his eyes from the manuscript. Grant Ames, III, was at the scotch again.

"You will be cut down eventually," Ellery said, "by a pickled liver."

"Killjoy," Ames said. "But at the moment I feel myself a part of history, son. An actor under the Great Proscenium."

"Drinking himself to death?"

"Bluenose. I'm talking of the manuscript. In the year 1888 Sherlock Holmes received a mysterious surgeon's kit. He trained his marvellous talents on it and began one of his marvellous adventures. Three-quarters of a century later, another package is delivered to another famous detective."

"What's your point?" grumbled Ellery, visibly torn between Dr. Watson's manuscript and the empty typewriter.

"All that remains to complete the historic re-run is to train the modern talent on the modern adventure. Proceed, my dear Ellery. I'll function as Watson."

Ellery squirmed.

"Of course, you may challenge my *bona fides*. In substantiation, I point out that I have followed the Master's career faithfully."

That pierced the fog. Ellery studied his guest distastefully. "Really? All right, wise guy. Quote: 'It was in the spring of the year 1894 and all London was interested, and the fashionable world dismayed, by the murder of the—'?"

"'Honourable Ronald Adair.' Unquote," said Ames promptly. *"The Adventure of the Empty House,* from *The Return of Sherlock Holmes."*

"Quote: 'She had drawn a little gleaming revolver and emptied barrel after barrel into—'"

"'—Milverton's body, the muzzle within two feet of his shirt-front.' Unquote. *The Adventure of Charles Augustus Milverton."*

"You scintillate, Watson! Quote: 'These are the trodden, but not the downtrodden. These are the lowly, but never the low.'"

"Unquote." The playboy yawned. "Your efforts to trap me are childish, my dear Ellery. You quoted yourself, from *The Player on the Other Side."*

Ellery scowled at him. The fellow was not all overstuffed blondes and expensive scotch. *"Touché, touché.* Now let's see—I'm sure I can stick you—"

"I'm sure you can if you stall long enough, but that's exactly what I'm not going to let you do. Go into your act, Mr. Queen. You've read the first chapter of the manuscript. If you don't come up with some Queenian deductions, I'll never borrow a book of yours again."

"All I can tell you at the moment is that the handwriting purporting to be Watson's is precise, firm, and a little crabbed."

"You don't sound like Holmes to me, old buddy. The question is, *is* it Watson's. Is the manuscript the McCoy? Come, come, Queen! Apply your powers."

"Oh, shut up," Ellery said, and he went on reading.

CHAPTER II

THE CASTLE ON THE MOOR

IN HIS LATTER life, as I have recorded elsewhere, my friend Sherlock Holmes retired from the feverish pace of London to keep bees, of all things, on the South Downs. He thus terminated his career with no regret whatever, turning to that husbandman's activity with the same single-mindedness that had enabled him to track down so many of the world's cleverest criminals.

But at the time Jack the Ripper stalked London's streets and by-ways, Holmes was a whole-hearted creature of urban life. His every faculty was keyed to the uncertainties of London's dawns and dusks. The sinister stench of a Soho alley could set his nostrils a-quiver, whilst the scent of spring stirring a rural countryside might well put him a-dozing.

It was therefore with surprise and pleasure that I witnessed his interest in the passing scene as the express hurtled us towards Devonshire that morning. He gazed through the window with a concentrated air, then suddenly straightened his thin shoulders.

"Ah, Watson! The sharp air of approaching winter. It is invigorating."

I for one found it not so at the moment, an atrocious cigar between the teeth of a dour old Scot, who had boarded with us, befouling the compartment. But Holmes seemed not to notice the reek. Outside, the leaves were turning, and flashes of autumnal colour streamed past.

26

"This England, Watson. This other Eden, demi-Paradise."

I recognised the near-quotation and was doubly surprised. I knew, certainly, of the sentimental streak in my friend, but he rarely allowed it to show through the fabric of his scientific nature. Yet, pride of birthright in the Briton is a national trait, and Holmes had not escaped it.

As our journey neared its destination, his cheerful mien vanished; he became pensive. We were on the moors, those broad stretches of mire and morass that cling like a great scab to England's face. As if Nature insisted upon a proper setting, the sun had vanished behind thick cloud-banks, and we seemed to have been plunged into a place of eternal twilight.

We soon found ourselves upon the platform of a small country station, where Holmes thrust his hands deep into his pockets, his deep-set eyes kindled, as they so often did when he was beset by a problem.

"Do you recall the affair of the Baskervilles, Watson, and the curse that darkened their lives?"

"Well do I!"

"We are not far from their holdings. But of course we go in the opposite direction."

"And just as well. That hound of Hell still haunts my dreams."

I was puzzled. Ordinarily, when Holmes was involved in a case, he viewed his surroundings single-mindedly, sharply aware of a bruised twig while remaining oblivious of the landscape in which it lay. At such times, reminiscence was no part of it. Now he stirred restlessly, as though he regretted having allowed impulse to send him upon our journey.

"Watson," said he, "let us arrange for the rental of a dog-cart, and get this business over with."

The pony we procured no doubt had relations among the ones that ran wild on the moors, but the little beast was tractable enough, and it clipped steadily away at the road between the village and the Shires estate.

After a time, the turrets of Shires Castle came into view, adding their tone of melancholy to the scene.

"The game-preserves are beyond," said Holmes. "The Duke has a variegated terrain." He scanned the country before us and added, "I doubt, Watson, that we shall find a jolly, red-cheeked host in that forbidding pile."

"Why do you say that?"

"People of long blood lines tend to reflect the colour of their surroundings. You will recall that there was not a single cheerful face at Baskerville Hall."

I did not dispute this, my attention being fixed upon the scowling grey of Shires Castle. It had once been complete with moat and drawbridge. However, more modern generations had come to depend for defence of life and limb upon the local constabulary. The moat had been filled in, and the bridgechains had not creaked for many a year.

We were ushered into a cold and cavernous drawing-room by a butler who took our names like Charon checking our passage across the Styx. I soon learned that Holmes's prediction had been accurate. The Duke of Shires was as icily forbidding a man as ever I had met.

He was of slight stature and gave the impression of being phthisical. It was an illusion. Upon closer inspection I saw a well-blooded face, and I sensed a wiry strength in his frail-appearing body.

The Duke did not invite us to be seated. Instead, he stated abruptly, "You were fortunate in finding me here. Another hour, and I should have been on my way to London. I spend little time here in the country. What is your business?"

Holmes's tone in no way reflected the ill-manners of the nobleman. "We will intrude upon your time no longer than is necessary, your Grace. We came merely to bring you this."

He proffered the surgeon's-kit, which we had wrapped in plain brown paper and secured with sealing wax.

"What is it?" said the Duke, not stirring.

"I suggest, your Grace," replied Holmes, "that you open it and discover for yourself."

With a frown, the Duke of Shires stripped off the wrappings. "Where did you get this?"

"I regret that I must first ask your Grace to identify it as your property."

"I have never seen it before. What earthly reason had you for bringing it to me?" The Duke had raised the lid and was staring at the instruments with what certainly appeared to be genuine bewilderment.

"If you will draw down the lining you will find our reason imprinted upon the leather underneath."

The Duke followed Holmes's suggestion still frowning. I was watching closely as he stared at the coat of arms and it was my turn to feel bewilderment. His expression changed. The palest of smiles touched his thin lips, his eyes brightened, and he regarded the case with a look I can only describe as one of intense satisfaction, almost of triumph. Then, as quickly, the look vanished.

I glanced at Holmes in search of some explanation, knowing that he would not have missed the nobleman's reaction. But the sharp eyes were hooded, the familiar face a mask. "I am sure your Grace's question is now answered," said Holmes.

"Of course," replied the Duke in casual tones, as though brushing the matter aside as of no consequence. "The case does not belong to me."

"Then perhaps your Grace could direct us to the owner?"

"My son, I presume. It no doubt belonged to Michael."

"It came from a London pawn-shop."

The Duke's lips curled in a cruel sneer. "I do not doubt it."

"Then if you will give us your son's address—"

"The son I refer to, Mr. Holmes, is *dead*. My younger, sir."

Holmes spoke gently. "I am indeed sorry to hear that, your Grace. Did he succumb to an illness?"

"A very great illness. He has been *dead* for six months."

The emphasis put by the nobleman upon the word "dead" struck me as odd. "Was your son a physician?" I inquired.

"He studied for the profession, but he failed at it, as he failed at everything. Then he *died*."

Again that strange emphasis. I glanced at Holmes, but he seemed more interested in the ponderous furnishings of the vaulted room, his glance darting here and there, his thin muscular hands clasped behind his back.

The Duke of Shires held forth the case. "As this is not my property, sir, I return it to you. And now, if you will excuse me, I must prepare for my journey."

I was puzzled by Holmes's behaviour. He had accepted the Duke's cavalier treatment without rancour. Holmes was not in the habit of allowing people to walk over him with hob-nail boots. His bow was deferential as he said, "We shall detain you no longer, your Grace."

The Duke's rude behaviour was consistent. He made no move to reach for the bell-rope that would have summoned the butler. Thus, we were compelled to find our way out as best we could, under his stare.

This proved a stroke of good fortune. We were crossing the baronial hall towards the outer portal, when two persons appeared through a side-entrance, a man and a child.

In contrast to the Duke, they did not seem at all hostile.

The child, a girl of nine or ten years of age, smiled as brightly as her little pallid face would permit. The man, like the Duke, was of slender build. His quick, liquid eyes, although they questioned, were merely curious. His dark resemblance to the Duke of Shires left room for but one conclusion. This was the other son.

It did not seem to me that their arrival was particularly startling, but it appeared to disconcert my friend Holmes. He came to a jerky halt, and the surgeon's-kit that he was carrying fell to the floor with a clatter of steel against stone that echoed through the great hall.

"How clumsy of me!" he exclaimed, and then proceeded to be even clumsier by blocking me off as I attempted to retrieve the instruments.

The man, with a smile, sprang into the breach. "Allow me, sir," said he, and went to his knees.

The child reacted almost as quickly. "Let me help you, Papa."

The man's smile glowed. "So you shall, my dear. We'll help the gentleman together. You may hand me the instruments. But carefully, lest you cut yourself."

We watched in silence as the little girl handed the shining implements to her father, one by one. His affection for her was touchingly apparent, his dark eyes hardly bearing to leave her as he swiftly returned the instruments to their proper niches.

When the business was finished, the man arose. But the little girl continued to scan the flag-stones upon which we stood. "The last one, Papa. Where did it go?"

"It appears to have been missing, dearest. I don't think it fell from the case." He glanced questioningly at Holmes, who came out of the brown study into which he contrived to have fallen.

"Indeed it was missing, sir. Thank you, and pardon my clumsiness."

"No harm done. I trust the instruments were not damaged." He handed the case to Holmes, who took it with a smile.

"Have I, perchance, the honour of addressing Lord Carfax?"

"Yes," the dark man said, pleasantly. "This is my daughter, Deborah."

"Allow me to present my colleague, Dr. Watson; I am Sherlock Holmes."

The name seemed to impress Lord Carfax; his eyes widened in surprise. "Dr. Watson," he murmured in acknowledgement, but his eyes remained on Holmes. "And you, sir—I am honoured indeed. I have read of your exploits."

"Your Lordship is too kind," replied Holmes.

Deborah's eyes sparkled. She curtsied and said, "I am honoured to meet you, too, sir." She spoke with a sweetness that was touching. Lord Carfax looked on proudly. Yet I sensed a sadness in his manner.

"Deborah," said he, gravely, "you must mark this as an event in your life, the day you met two famous gentlemen."

"Indeed I shall, Papa," replied the little girl, solemnly dutiful. She had heard of neither of us, I was quite certain.

Holmes concluded the amenities by saying, "We called, your Lordship, to return this case to the Duke of Shires, whom we believed to be its rightful owner."

"And you discovered that you were in error."

"Quite. His Grace thought that it had probably belonged to your deceased brother, Michael Osbourne."

"Deceased?" It was more of a tired comment than a question.

"That was what we were given to understand."

Sadness appeared clearly in Lord Carfax's face. "That may or may not be true. My father, Mr. Holmes, is a stern and unforgiving man, which you no doubt surmised. To him, the good name of Osbourne stands above all else. Keeping the Shires escutcheon free of blemish is a passion with him. When he disowned my younger brother some six months ago, he pronounced Michael dead." He paused to sigh. "I fear Michael will remain dead, so far as Father is concerned, even though he may still live."

"Are you yourself aware," asked Holmes, "whether your brother is alive or dead?"

Lord Carfax frowned, looking remarkably like the Duke. When he spoke, I thought I detected evasiveness in his voice. "Let me say, sir, that I have no actual proof of his death."

"I see," replied Holmes. Then he looked down at Deborah Osbourne and smiled. The little girl came forward and put her hand into his.

"I like you very much, sir," said she gravely.

It was a charming moment. Holmes appeared embarrassed by this open-hearted confession. Her small hand remained in his as he said, "Granted, Lord Carfax, that your father is an unbending man. Still, to disown a son! A decision such as that is not made lightly. Your brother's transgression must indeed have been a serious one."

"Michael married against my father's wishes." Lord Carfax shrugged his shoulders. "I am not in the habit, Mr. Holmes, of discussing my family's affairs with strangers, but—" he touched his daughter's shining head "—Deborah is my barometer of character." I thought his Lordship was going to ask what Holmes's interest in Michael Osbourne was based upon, but he did not.

Holmes, too, appeared to have expected such a question. When it did not come, he extended the surgical-

33

case. "Perhaps you would like to have this, your Lordship."

Lord Carfax took the case with a silent bow.

"And now—our train will not wait, I fear—we must be off." Holmes looked down from his great height. "Goodbye, Deborah. Meeting you is the most agreeable thing that has happened to Dr. Watson and me in a very long time."

"I hope you will come again, sir," replied the child. "It gets so lonely here when Papa is away."

Holmes said little as we drove back to the village. He scarcely replied to my comments, and it was not until we were flying back towards London that he invited conversation. His lean features set in that abstracted look I knew so well, he said, "An interesting man, Watson."

"Perhaps," I replied, tartly. "But also as repulsive a one as ever I care to meet. It is men of his calibre—they are few, thank heaven!—who stain the reputation of the British nobility."

My indignation amused Holmes. "I was referring to *filius* rather than *pater*."

"The son? I was touched by Lord Carfax's evident love for his daughter, of course—"

"But you felt he was too informative?"

"That was exactly my impression, Holmes, although I don't see how you became aware of it. I did not enter into the conversation."

"Your face is like a mirror, my dear Watson," said he.

"Even he admitted that he talked too freely about his family's personal affairs."

"But did he? Let us assume him, first, to be a stupid man. In that case he becomes a loving father with an over-large oral cavity."

"But if we assume him, with more difficulty, to be not stupid at all?"

34

"Then he created precisely the image he wished to, which I incline to believe. He knew me by name and reputation, and you, Watson. I strongly doubt that he accepted us as mere Good Samaritans, come all this way to restore an old surgeon's-kit to its rightful owner."

"Should that necessarily loosen his tongue?"

"My dear fellow, he told us nothing that I did not already know, or could not have discovered with ease in the files of any London daily."

"Then what was it that he did not reveal?"

"Whether his brother Michael is dead or alive. Whether he is in contact with his brother."

"I assumed, from what he said, that he does not know."

"That, Watson, may have been what he wished you to assume." Before I could reply, Holmes went on. "As it happens, I did not go to Shires uninformed. Kenneth Osbourne, the lineal Duke, had two sons. Michael, the younger, of course inherited no title. Whether or not this instilled jealousy in him I do not know, but he so conducted himself thenceforward as to earn the sobriquet, from the journalists of London, of The Wild One. You spoke of his father's brutal sternness, Watson. To the contrary, the record reveals the Duke as having been amazingly lenient with his younger son. The boy finally tried his father's patience too far when he married a woman of the oldest profession; in fine, a prostitute."

"I begin to see," muttered I. "Out of spite, or hatred, to besmirch the title he could not inherit."

"Perhaps," said Holmes. "In any case, it would have been difficult for the Duke to assume otherwise."

"I did not know," said I, humbly.

"It is human, my dear Watson, to side with the under-dog. But it is wise to discover beforehand exactly who the under-dog is. In the case of the Duke, I grant that he is a difficult man, but he bears a cross."

I replied, with some despair, "Then I suppose my evaluation of Lord Carfax is faulty, also."

"I do not know, Watson. We have very little data. However, he did fail on two accounts."

"I was not aware of it."

"Nor was he."

My mind was centred upon a broader prospect. "Holmes," said I, "this whole affair is curiously unsatisfactory. Surely this journey was not motivated by a simple desire on your part to restore lost property?"

He gazed out of the carriage-window. "The surgeon's-kit was delivered to our door. I doubt we were mistaken for a lost-and-found bureau."

"But by whom was it sent?"

"By someone who wished us to have it."

"Then we can only wait."

"Watson, to say that I smell a devious purpose here is no doubt fanciful. But the stench is strong. Perhaps you will get your wish."

"My wish?"

"I believe you recently suggested that I give the Yard some assistance in the case of Jack the Ripper."

"Holmes—!"

"Of course there is no evidence to connect the Ripper with the surgeon's-kit. But the post-mortem knife is missing."

"The implication has not escaped me. Why, this very night it may be plunged into the body of some unfortunate!"

"A possibility, Watson. The removal of the scalpel may have been symbolical, a subtle allusion to the fiendish stalker."

"Why did the sender not come forward?"

"There could be any number of reasons. I should put fear high on the list. In time, I think, we shall know the truth."

Holmes lapsed into the preoccupation I knew so well. Further probing on my part, I knew, would have been useless. I sat back and stared gloomily out the window as the train sped towards Paddington.

Ellery Tries

ELLERY LOOKED up from the notebook.

Grant Ames, finishing his nth drink, asked eagerly, "Well?"

Ellery got up and went to a bookshelf, frowning. He took a book down and searched for something while Grant waited. He returned the book to the shelf and came back.

"Christianson's."

Grant looked blank.

"According to the reference there, Christianson's was a well-known stationery manufacturer of the period. Their watermark is on the paper of the notebook."

"That does it, then!"

"Not necessarily. Anyway, there's no point in trying to authenticate the manuscript. If someone's trying to sell it to me, I'm not buying. If it's genuine, I can't afford it. If it's a phony—"

"I don't think that was the idea, old boy."

"Then what was the idea?"

"How should I know? I suppose someone wants you to read it."

Ellery pulled his nose fretfully. "You're sure it was put into your car at that party?"

"Had to be."

"And it was addressed by a woman. How many women were there?"

Grant counted on his fingers. "Four."

"Any bookworms? Collectors? Librarians? Little old ladies smelling of lavender sachets and must?"

"Hell, no. Four slick young chicks trying to look seductive. After a husband. Frankly, Ellery, I can't conceive one of them knowing Sherlock Holmes from Aristophanes. But with your kooky talents, you could stalk the culprit in an afternoon."

"Look, Grant, any other time and I'd play the game. But I told you. I'm in one of my periodic binds. I simply haven't the time."

"Then it ends here, Maestro? For God's sake, man, what are you, a hack? Here I toss a delicious mystery into your lap—"

"And I," said Ellery, firmly placing the notebook in Grant Ames's lap, "toss it right back to you. I have a suggestion. *You* rush out, glass in hand, and track down your lady joker."

"I might at that," whined the millionaire.

"Fine. Let me know."

"The manuscript didn't grip you?"

"Of course it does." Reluctantly, Ellery picked up the journal and riffled through it.

"That's my old buddy!" Ames rose. "Why don't I leave it here? After all, it is addressed to you. I could report back at intervals—"

"Make it long intervals."

"Mine host. All right, I'll bother you as little as I can."

"Less, if possibly. And now will you beat it, Grant? I'm serious."

"What you are, friend, is grim. No fun at all." Ames turned in the doorway. "Oh, by the way, order some more scotch. You've run out."

When he was alone again, Ellery stood indecisively. Finally he put the notebook down on the sofa and went to his desk. He stared at the keys. The keys stared

39

back. He shifted in his swivel chair; his bottom was itching. He pulled the chair closer. He pulled his nose again.

The notebook lay quietly on the sofa.

Ellery ran a sheet of blank paper into the machine. He raised his hands, flexed his fingers, thought, and began to type.

He typed rapidly, stopped, and read what he had written:

"The Lord," said Nikki, "choves a leerful giver."

"All *right!*" said Ellery. "Just one more chapter!"

He jumped up and ran to the sofa and grabbed the notebook and opened it and began to devour Chapter III.

CHAPTER III

WHITECHAPEL

"BY THE WAY, Holmes, whatever became of Wiggins?"
I asked the question late the following morning in the
rooms at Baker Street.

We had had a buffet supper the previous evening at the
station after our return from Shires Castle, whereupon
Holmes had said, "The young American pianist, Benton,
plays at Albert Hall tonight. I recommend him highly,
Watson."

"I was not aware that the States had produced any great
pianoforte talents."

Holmes had laughed. "Come, come, my dear fellow! Let
the Americans go. It has been more than a century now,
and they have been doing quite well over there."

"You wish me to accompany you? I should be delighted."

"I was suggesting the concert for your evening. I have
a few investigations in mind which are better made at
night."

"In that case, I prefer the easy-chair by the fire and one
of your fascinating books."

"I recommend one I recently acquired, *Uncle Tom's
Cabin*, by an American lady named Stowe. A lugubrious
work, meant to stir the nation to correct a great injustice.
It was, I believe, one of the causes of the War Between
the States. Well, I must be off. Perhaps I shall join you in
a night-cap later."

Holmes, however, returned very late, after I was abed.

He did not awaken me, so that our next meeting was at breakfast. I hoped for an account of his night's work, but none was forthcoming. Nor did he appear to be in haste to get on with things, lounging lazily in his mouse-coloured dressing-gown over his tea and clouding the room with heavy exhalations from his beloved clay pipe.

Came a sudden clatter upon the stairs, and there rushed into the room a dozen of the dirtiest, most ragged urchins in all London. They were Holmes's incredible band of street Arabs, whom he called variously "the Baker Street division of the detective police force," his "unofficial force," and "the Baker Street irregulars."

" 'Tention!" snapped Holmes; and the urchins struggled into a ragged line and presented their begrimed little faces in what they evidently took to be a military posture.

"Now, have you found it?"

"Yes, sir, we 'ave," replied one of the band.

"It was me, sir!" cut in another eagerly as he grinned, showing gaps where three teeth were wanting.

"Very good," said Holmes, sternly, "but we work as a unit. No individual glory, men. One for all and all for one."

"Yes, *sir*," came the chorus.

"The report?"

"It's in Whitechapel."

"Ah!"

"On Great Heapton Street, near the pass-over. The street is narrow there, sir."

"Very good," said Holmes again. "Here is your pay. Now be off with you."

He gave each urchin a shining shilling. They clattered happily away, as they had come, and we soon heard their shrill young voices from below.

Now Holmes knocked the dottle from his pipe. "Wiggins? Oh, he did very well. Joined her Majesty's forces. My last note from him was post-marked Africa."

"He was a sharp youngster, as I recall."

"So are they all. And London's supply of the little beggars never diminishes. But I have an inquiry to make. Let us be off."

It took no feat of intellect to predict our destination. So I was not surprised when we stood before a pawnshop window on Great Heapton Street, in Whitechapel. The street, as Holmes had deduced and the urchins confirmed, was narrow, with high buildings on the side opposite the shop. When we arrived, the sun was just cutting a line across the glass, the inscription upon which read: *Joseph Beck—Loans.*

Holmes pointed to the display in the window. "The kit sat there, Watson. Do you see where the sun strikes?"

I could only nod my head. Accustomed though I was to the unerring keenness of his judgements, the proof never ceased to amaze me.

Inside the shop, we were greeted by a pudgy man of middle-age whose moustaches were heavily waxed and drilled into military points. Joseph Beck was the archetype of German tradesmen, and his efforts to produce a Prussian effect were ludicrous.

"May I be of service, sirs?" His English was thickly accented.

I presume, in that neighbourhood, we were a cut above his usual run of clients; possibly he hoped to acquire a pledge of high value. He actually clicked his heels and came to attention.

"A friend," said Holmes, "recently made me a gift, a surgeon's-case purchased in your shop."

Herr Beck's protuberant little eyes turned sly. "Yes?"

"But one of the instruments was missing from the case. I should like to complete the set. Do you have some surgical instruments from which I might select the missing one?"

"I am afraid, sir, I cannot help you." The pawnbroker was clearly disappointed.

"Do you recall the set I refer to, the transaction?"

"*Ach*, yes, sir. It took place a week ago, and I get very few such articles. But the set was complete when the woman redeemed it and carried it away. Did she tell you one of the instruments was missing?"

"I do not recall," Holmes said, in an off-hand manner. "The point is that you cannot help me now."

"I am sorry, sir. I have no surgical instruments of any description."

Holmes pretended petulance. "All the way down here for nothing! You have caused me great inconvenience, Beck."

The man looked astonished. "You are being unreasonable, sir. I do not see how I am responsible for what occurred after the case left my shop."

Holmes shrugged his shoulders. "I suppose not," said he, carelessly. "But it is a nuisance. I came a long distance."

"But, sir, if you had inquired of the poor creature who redeemed the set—"

"The poor creature? I don't understand."

The severity of Holmes's tone frightened the man. With the tradesman's instinct to please, he hastened to apologise. "Forgive me, sir. My heart went out to the woman. In fact, I let her have the case at a too generous price. Her terribly disfigured face has haunted me."

"Ah," murmured Holmes. "I see." He was turning away in clever disappointment when his hawk's-face brightened. "A thought occurs to me. The man who originally pledged the case—if I could get in touch with him..."

"I doubt it, sir. It was some time ago."

"How long?"

"I would have to consult my ledger."

Frowning, he produced a ledger from underneath the counter and thumbed through it. "Here it is. Why, it has been almost four months. How time flies!"

"Quite," agreed Holmes, drily. "You have the name and address of the man?"

"It was not a man, sir. It was a lady."

Holmes and I glanced at each other. "I see," said Holmes. "Well, even after four months, it might still be worth an effort. What is her name, pray?"

The pawnbroker peered at his ledger. "Young. Miss Sally Young."

"Her address?"

"The Montague Street Hostel."

"Odd place of residence," I ventured.

"Yes, *mein Herr*. It is in the heart of Whitechapel. A dangerous place these days."

"Indeed it is. Good-day to you," said Holmes, civilly. "You have been most accommodating."

As we walked away from the pawnshop, Holmes laughed softly. "A type who must be adroitly handled, this Joseph Beck. One can lead him great distances, but he cannot be pushed an inch."

"I thought he cooperated handsomely."

"Indeed he did. But the least odour of officialdom in our inquiry and we should not have pried the time of day out of him."

"Your theory that the scalpel was removed as a purely symbolic gesture, Holmes, has been proved correct."

"Perhaps, though the fact is of no great value. But now, a visit to the Montague Street Hostel and Miss Sally Young seems in order. I'm sure you have formed opinions as to the stations of the two females we are seeking?"

"Of course. The one who pawned the set was clearly in straitened financial circumstances."

"A possibility, Watson, though far from a certainty."

"If not, why did she pledge the set?"

"I am inclined to think it was a service she rendered a second party. Someone who was unable or did not care to appear personally at the pawn-shop. A surgeon's-kit is hardly an article one would expect to find a lady owning. And as to the woman who redeemed the pledge?"

"We know nothing of her except that she sustained some injury to her face. Perhaps she is a victim of the Ripper, who escaped death at his hands?"

"Capital, Watson! An admirable hypothesis. However, the point that struck me involves something a little different. You will remember that Herr Beck referred to the one who redeemed the case as a *woman*, while he spoke in a more respectful tone of the pledger as a *lady*. Hence, we are safe in assuming that Miss Sally Young is a person to command some respect."

"Of course, Holmes. The implications, I am frank to admit, escaped me."

"The redeemer is no doubt of a lower order. She could well be a prostitute. Certainly this neighbourhood abounds with such unfortunates."

Montague Street lay at no great distance; it was less than a twenty-minute walk from the pawn-shop. It proved to be a short thoroughfare connecting Purdy Court and Olmstead Circus, the latter being well-known as a refuge for London's swarms of beggars. We turned into Montague Street and had progressed only a few steps when Holmes halted. "Aha! What have we here?"

My glance followed his to a sign over an archway of ancient stone, displaying a single word, *Mortuary*. I do not see myself as especially sensitive, but as I gazed into the murky depths of the tunnel-like entrance, the same depression of spirit came over me that I had experienced at first sight of the Shires castle.

46

"This is no hostel, Holmes," said I. "Unless a sanctuary for the dead can be called such!"

"Let us suspend judgement until we investigate," replied he; and he pushed open a creaking door that led into a cobbled courtyard.

"There is the smell of death here, without a doubt," said I.

"And very recent death, Watson. Else why should our friend Lestrade be on the premises?"

Two men stood in conversation at the far side of the courtyard, and Holmes had identified the one of them more quickly than I. It was indeed Inspector Lestrade of Scotland Yard, even leaner and more ferret-like than I recalled him.

Lestrade turned at the tramp of our footsteps. An expression of surprise came over his face. "Mr. 'Olmes! What are you doing here?"

"How good to see you, Lestrade!" exclaimed Holmes, with a warm smile. "It is heartening to find Scotland Yard dutifully following where crime leads."

"You needn't be sarcastic," grumbled Lestrade.

"Nerves, man? Something seems to have you by the short hairs."

"If you don't know what it is, you didn't read the paper this morning," said Lestrade, shortly.

"As a matter of fact, I did not."

The police officer turned to acknowledge my presence. "Dr. Watson. It has been a long time since our paths crossed."

"Far too long, Inspector Lestrade. You are well, I trust?"

"A bit of lumbago now and again. I'll survive." Then he added darkly, "At least until I see this Whitechapel maniac dragged to the gallows."

"The Ripper again?" asked Holmes, sharply.

"The very same. The fourth attack, Mr. 'Olmes. You

47

have, of course, read about him, although I haven't heard of you coming 'round to offer your services."

Holmes did not parry the thrust. Instead, his eyes flicked in my direction. "We draw closer, Watson."

"What was that?" exclaimed Lestrade.

"The fourth, you said? No doubt you mean the fourth *official* murder?"

"Official or not, 'Olmes—"

"What I meant was that you cannot be sure. You have found the bodies of four of the Ripper's victims. But others may have been dismembered and thoroughly disposed of."

"A cheerful thought," muttered Lestrade.

"This 'fourth' victim. I should like to view the body."

"Inside. Oh, this is Dr. Murray. He is in charge here."

Dr. Murray was a cadaverous man, with a deathlike complexion, and a poised manner which impressed me favourably. His attitude reflected the inner resignation one often finds in those who deal intimately with the dead. He acknowledged Lestrade's introduction with a bow, and said, "I do officiate here, but I had rather posterity remembered me as director of the hostel next door. It affords greater opportunity for service. The poor creatures who come here are beyond it."

"Let's get on with it," interrupted Lestrade, and conducted us through a door. A strong carbolic-acid odour greeted us, an odour I had grown to know too well in her Majesty's Indian service.

The room into which we were shown demonstrated how little is ever done to confer dignity upon the dead. It was less a room than a long, wide passageway, each inch of whose walls and ceiling was tastelessly whitewashed. One entire side consisted of a raised platform, upon which rude wooden tables jutted out at intervals. Fully half the

48

tables were occupied by sheeted, still figures; but Lestrade led us to the far end.

There, another platform stood, with its table and sheeted morsel of humanity. This platform was slightly higher, and so placed that a sign, *The Corpse for To-day*, might well have seemed appropriate.

"Annie Chapman," said Lestrade, morosely. "The latest victim of our butcher." With that, he drew back the sheet.

Holmes was the most objective of men where crime was concerned, but a grim pity invaded his face. And I must confess that I—accustomed to death both in the bed and upon the battlefield—was sickened. The girl had been slaughtered like an animal.

To my amazement, I saw what appeared to be disappointment supplant the pity upon Holmes's face. "The face is not scarred," he murmured, as if in complaint.

"The Ripper does not mutilate the faces of his victims," said Lestrade. "He confines his attentions to the more private parts of the body."

Holmes had turned cold and analytical. He could now have been regarding a specimen in a dissection-room. He touched my arm. "Note the skill of this unholy work, Watson. It verifies what we have read in the journals. The fiend does not cut at random."

Inspector Lestrade was scowling. "There is certainly nothing skilful in that slash across the abdomen, 'Olmes. The Ripper used a butcher's cleaver for that one."

"Before the abdomen was dissected, possibly with a surgeon's scalpel," muttered Holmes.

Lestrade shrugged his shoulders. "That second blow, the one to the heart. It was done by a cleaver, also."

"The left breast was removed with consummate skill, Lestrade," said I with a shudder.

"The Ripper's surgery varies. Its skill seems to depend

49

upon the time that is available to him. In some cases there has been scarcely any, cases in which he was interrupted in his devil's work."

"I am compelled to alter certain superficial ideas I had formed." Holmes appeared to be speaking to himself rather than to us. "A madman, certainly. But a clever one. Perhaps a brilliant one."

"Then you admit, Mr. 'Olmes, that the Yard is contending with no blundering idiot?"

"Most assuredly, Lestrade. And I shall be happy to give you whatever aid my limited powers allow."

This widened Lestrade's eyes. He had never before heard Holmes deprecate his own talents. The policeman searched for a suitable rejoinder, but apparently such was his astonishment that he could find none.

He recovered sufficiently, however, to voice his standard plaint. "And if you are lucky enough to apprehend the fiend—"

"I seek no credit, Lestrade," said Holmes. "Rest assured the Yard shall reap the glory." He paused, then added, gloomily, "If there is any." He turned to Dr. Murray. "I wonder if we may be permitted to inspect your hostel, Doctor?"

Dr. Murray bowed. "I should be honoured, Mr. Holmes."

At that moment a door opened, and a pathetic figure appeared. There was much about the shuffling creature to pity, but I was struck first by the total vacancy in his eyes. The expressionless features, the sagging, partially-open mouth, bespoke an idiot. The man shuffled forward and stepped upon the platform. He cast a look of empty inquiry at Dr. Murray, who smiled as one smiles at a child.

"Ah, Pierre. You may cover the body."

A spark of eagerness appeared on that vacuous countenance. I could not help thinking of a faithful dog given a chore by a kindly master. Then Dr. Murray gestured, and we moved away from the platform.

"I'll be off," said Lestrade, sniffing wrinkle-nosed at the carbolic. "If there is any information you require, Mr. 'Olmes," said he, politely, "do not hesitate to call upon me."

"Thank you, Lestrade," said Holmes with equal courtesy. The two detectives had evidently decided to call a truce until the morbid affair could be resolved—the first such truce between them, I might add, that ever I was aware of.

As we quitted the charnel-house, I glanced back and saw Pierre smoothing the sheet carefully over the body of Annie Chapman. Holmes, I noted, also glanced in the simpleton's direction, and something kindled in his grey eyes.

CHAPTER IV

DR. MURRAY'S HOSTEL

"ONE DOES WHAT one can," said Dr. Murray, a few moments later, "but, in a city of the size of London, it is a little like trying to sweep back the sea with a broom. A sea of destitution and despair."

We had left the morgue, and crossed a flag-stoned inner courtyard. He ushered us through another door, and into a shabby but more cheerful atmosphere. The hostel was very old. It had been built originally as a stable, a long, low, stone building with the places for the stalls still clearly marked. Again, buckets of whitewash had been used, but the eternal odour of the carbolic was here mingled with a slightly less disagreeable effluvium of medicines, steaming vegetable stew, and unbathed bodies. As the building extended onward in railway fashion, the stalls had been fashioned into larger units, double and sometimes triple their original size, and put to appropriate uses. Black-lettered cards identified them variously as dormitories for women and men. There was a dispensary, and a clinical waiting-room with stone benches. Ahead of us, a sign read: *This Way to Chapel and Dining-Hall.*

Curtains had been drawn across the entrance to the women's dormitory, but that of the men stood open, and several sorry-looking derelicts slept upon their iron cots.

In the clinical area, three patients awaited attention, while the dispensary was occupied by a huge, brutish man who looked freshly come from sweeping a chimney. He was seated, a sullen scowl upon his face. His eyes were fastened upon a pretty young lady ministering to him. One of his vast feet rested upon a low stool; the young lady had just finished bandaging it. She came up from her knees and brushed a lock of dark hair back from her forehead.

"He cut it badly upon a shard of broken glass," she told Dr. Murray. The doctor stooped to inspect the bandage, giving the brute's foot no less attention than it would have received in any Harley Street surgery. He straightened and spoke kindly.

"You must come back to-morrow and have the dressing changed, my friend. Be sure, now."

The oaf was entirely without gratitude. "I can't put my boot on. 'Ow am I goin' to get about?"

He spoke as though the doctor were responsible, with such surliness that I could not restrain myself. "If you had stayed sober, my good man, perhaps you could have avoided the broken glass."

"'Ere now, guv'ner!" says he, bold as brass. "A man's got to 'ave a pint once in a while!"

"I doubt if you've ever held yourself to a pint."

"Please wait here a few moments," interposed Dr. Murray, "I'll have Pierre bring you a stick. We keep a small stock for emergencies."

Turning to the young lady, he went on, "Sally, these gentlemen are Mr. Sherlock Holmes and his colleague, Dr. Watson. Gentlemen, this is Miss Sally Young, my niece and good right arm. I don't know what the hostel would be without her."

Sally Young extended a slim hand to each of us in turn. "I am honoured," said she, cool and self-possessed. "I have heard both names before. But I never expected to meet such famous personages."

"You are too kind," murmured Holmes.

53

Her tact in including me, a mere shadow to Sherlock Holmes, was gracious, and I bowed.

Said Dr. Murray, "I'll get the stick myself, Sally. Will you conduct Mr. Holmes and Dr. Watson the rest of the way? Perhaps they would like to see the chapel and the kitchen."

"Certainly. This way, please."

Dr. Murray hurried away in the direction of the morgue, and we followed Miss Young. But only for a short distance. Before we reached the door, Holmes said abruptly, "Our time is limited, Miss Young. Perhaps the tour can be finished during another visit. We are here to-day for professional reasons."

The girl seemed not to be surprised. "I understand, Mr. Holmes. Is there something I can do?"

"Perhaps there is. Some time ago you pledged a certain article in a pawn-shop on Great Heapton Street. Do you recall?"

With no hesitation whatever, she replied, "Of course. It was not so long ago as that."

"Would you object to telling us how you came by the case, and why you pledged it?"

"Not at all. It belonged to Pierre."

I thought this startling news, but Holmes did not move a muscle. "The poor fellow who has lost his wits."

"A pitiful case," said the girl.

"A hopeless one, I venture to say," said Holmes. "We met him a few minutes ago. Could you enlighten us as to his background?"

"We know nothing about him prior to his arrival here. But that arrival, I must say, was dramatic. I came through the morgue late one night, and found him standing beside one of the corpses."

"Doing what, Miss Young?"

"He was doing nothing whatever, merely standing by

54

the body in the confused state you must surely have noticed. I approached him and brought him to my uncle. He has been here ever since. The police were evidently not seeking him, for Inspector Lestrade has shown no interest in him whatever."

My opinion of Miss Sally Young went higher. Here was courage indeed. A girl who could walk at night about a charnel-house, see a gargoyle figure such as Pierre's standing over one of the corpses, and not flee in terror!

"That's hardly a criterion," began Holmes, and stopped.

"I beg your pardon, sir?"

"A random thought, Miss Young. Please proceed."

"We came to the opinion that someone had guided Pierre to the hostel and left him, as unwed mothers leave their infants at the door of a sanctuary. Dr. Murray examined him, and found that he had once sustained a terrible injury, as if he had been brutally beaten. The wounds about his head had healed, but nothing could be done to dispel the mists that had permanently settled over his brain. He has proved to be harmless, and he is so pathetically eager to help about the place that he has made his own berth. We of course would not dream of sending him back into a world with which he cannot cope."

"And the surgeon's-kit?"

"He had a bundle with him, containing wearing apparel. The kit was buried in their midst, the only thing of value he possessed."

"What did he tell you of himself?"

"Nothing. He speaks only with effort, single words which are hardly intelligible."

"But his name—Pierre?"

She laughed, an attractive touch of colour coming into her cheeks. "I took the liberty of baptising him. What clothing he carried bore French labels. And there was a coloured handkerchief with French script interwoven in the cloth. Thus, and for no other reason, I began calling him Pierre, although I feel sure he is not French."

"How did you happen to pawn the case?" asked Holmes.

"That came about quite simply. As I have told you, Pierre brought virtually nothing with him, and our funds at the hostel are severely allocated. We were in no position to outfit Pierre properly. So I thought of the surgical-case. It was clearly of value, and he could have no need of it. I explained to him what I proposed, and to my surprise he nodded violently." She paused here to laugh. "The only difficulty was in getting him to accept the proceeds. He wanted to put it into the general fund of the hostel."

"Then he is still capable of emotion. At least of gratitude."

"Indeed he is," replied Sally Young, warmly. "And now perhaps, sir, you will answer a question of mine. Why are you interested in the surgeon's-kit?"

"It was sent to me by an unknown person."

Her eyes widened. "Then someone redeemed it!"

"Yes. Have you any idea who that person might have been?"

"Not in the least." After a thoughtful pause, she said, "There does not necessarily have to be a connection. I mean, someone could have come upon the case and redeemed it as a bargain."

"One of the instruments was missing when it reached me."

"That is odd! I wonder what could have happened to it."

"The set was complete when you pledged it?"

"Indeed it was."

"Thank you, Miss Young."

At that moment the door before us opened; a man came through. And, although Lord Carfax was perhaps not the last person I expected to see, he was certainly not the first.

"Your Lordship," exclaimed Holmes. "Our paths cross again."

Lord Carfax was as surprised as I. Indeed, he seemed utterly discomposed. It was Sally Young who broke the silence. "Your Lordship has met these gentlemen?"

"We had that privilege only yesterday," said Holmes. "At the Duke of Shires's residence."

Lord Carfax found his voice. "Mr. Holmes refers to my father's country-home." Then, turning back to Holmes, he said, "This is a far more likely place for me to be than for you gentlemen. I spend a good deal of my time here."

"Lord Carfax is our angel from Heaven," said Sally Young rapturously. "He has given of his money and of his time so generously, that the hostel is as much his as ours. It could hardly exist without him."

Lord Carfax flushed. "You make too much of it, my dear."

She laid an affectionate hand upon his arm; her eyes were very bright. Then the glow faded; her whole manner changed. "Lord Carfax. There is another one. Have you heard?"

He nodded, sombrely. "I wonder if it will ever end! Mr. Holmes, are you by any chance applying your talents to the hunt for the Ripper?"

"We shall see what develops," said Holmes, abruptly. "We have taken up enough of your time, Miss Young. I trust that we shall meet again."

With that we bowed and departed, going out through the silent morgue, that was now deserted except for the dead.

Night had fallen, and the street-lamps of Whitechapel dotted the lonely thoroughfares, deepening rather than banishing the shadows.

I drew up my collar. "I don't mind saying, Holmes, that a good fire and a cup of hot tea—"

"On guard, Watson!" cried Holmes, his reactions far sharper than my own; and an instant later we were fighting for our lives. Three toughs had leapt out of the darkness of a courtyard and were upon us.

I saw the flash of a knife-blade as one of them shouted, "You two take the big cove!" Thus I was left with the third thug, but he was quite enough, armed as he was with a glittering weapon. The savagery of his attack left no doubt as to his intentions. I whirled to meet his attack not an instant too soon. But my stick slipped from my grasp, and I would have gone down with the brute's blade in my flesh if he had not slipped in his eagerness to get at me. He fell forward, pawing the air, and I acted from instinct, bringing my knee upwards. A welcome bolt of pain shot up my thigh as my knee-cap connected with my assailant's face. He bellowed in pain and staggered back, blood spouting from his nose.

Holmes had retained his stick and his wits. From the corner of my eye I witnessed his first defensive move. Using the stick as a sword, he thrust straight and true at the nearest man's abdomen. The ferrule sank deep, bringing a scream of agony from the man and sending him down, clutching his belly.

That was all I saw, because my assailant was up and at me again. I got my fingers around the wrist of his knife-arm and veered the blade off its course towards my throat. Then we were locked together, struggling desperately. We went to the cobble-stones in a frantic sprawl. He was a big man, strongly-muscled, and even though I strained against his arm with every ounce of my strength, the blade moved closer to my throat.

I was in the act of consigning my soul to its Maker when a thud of Holmes's stick glazed the eyes of my would-be murderer and pitched him over my head. With an effort I heaved off the weight of the man's body, and

58

struggled to my knees. At that moment there was a cry of rage and pain from one of Holmes's assailants. One of them cried, "Come on, Butch! These blokes are a bit thick!" and, with that, my attacker was snatched to his feet, the trio ran off into the shadows, and disappeared.

Holmes was kneeling beside me. "Watson! Are you all right? Did that knife get into you?"

"Not so much as a scratch, Holmes," I assured him.

"If you'd been hurt, I should never have forgiven myself."

"Are *you* all right, old chap?"

"Except for a bruised shin." Helping me to my feet, Holmes added grimly, "I am an idiot. An attack was the last thing I anticipated. The aspects of this case change swiftly."

"Don't blame yourself. How could you possibly have known?"

"It is my business to know."

"You were alert enough to beat them at their own game, when every advantage was on their side."

But Holmes would not be comforted. "I am slow, slow, Watson," said he. "Come, we shall find a hansom and get you home to that fire and a hot tea."

A cab hove in sight and picked us up. When we were rattling back towards Baker Street, Holmes said, "It would be interesting to know who sent them."

"Obviously, someone who wishes us dead," was my retort.

"But our ill-wisher, whoever he is, appears to have used poor judgement in selecting his emissaries. He should have chosen cooler heads. Their enthusiasm for the job impaired their efficiency."

"Our good fortune, Holmes."

"They achieved one goal, at least. If there was any doubt before, they have wedded me irrevocably to this case."

Holmes's tone was grim indeed, and we rode the remainder of the journey in silence. It was not until we were seated before the fire with steaming cups of Mrs. Hudson's tea that he spoke again.

"After I left you yesterday, Watson, I corroborated a few small points. Did you know that a nude—a quite good work, by the way—by one Kenneth Osbourne, hangs in the National Gallery?"

"Kenneth Osbourne, did you say?" I exclaimed.

"The Duke of Shires."

Ellery Succeeds

HE HAD TYPED steadily through the night; dawn found him blinking, stubbled, and famished.

Ellery went into the kitchen and opened the refrigerator and brought out a bottle of milk and the three sandwiches he had failed to eat the previous afternoon. He wolfed them down, drained what was left of the milk, wiped his mouth, yawned, stretched, and went to the phone.

"Morning, dad. Who won?"

"Who won what?" Inspector Queen asked querulously, from Bermuda.

"The horseshoe game."

"Oh, that. They rang in some stacked shoes on me. How's the weather in New York? Lousy, I hope."

"The weather?" Ellery glanced at the window, but the Venetian blinds were closed. "To tell you the truth, dad, I don't know. I worked all night."

"And you sent me down here for a rest! Son, why don't you join me?"

"I can't. It's not only this book I've got to finish, but Grant Ames dropped in yesterday. He drank me dry and left a package."

"Oh?" said the Inspector, coming to life. "What kind of package?"

Ellery told him.

The old man snorted. "Of all the baloney. Somebody's pulling a funny on you. Did you read it?"

"A few chapters. I must say it's pretty well done. Fascinating, in fact. But then—out of nowhere—lightning struck, and I got back to my typewriter. How do you plan to spend your day, dad?"

"Frying myself on that damned beach. Ellery, I'm so bored I'm beginning to chew my nails. Son, *won't* you let me come home?"

"Not a chance," said Ellery. "You fry. Tell you what. How would you like to read an unpublished Sherlock Holmes?"

Inspector Queen's voice took on a cunning note. "Say, that's an idea. I'll call the airline and book a stray seat—I can be in New York in no time—"

"Nothing doing. I'll mail the manuscript down to you."

"To hell with the manuscript!" howled his father.

"So long, daddy," said Ellery. "Don't forget to wear your dark glasses on the beach. And you eat everything they put on your plate."

He hung up hastily, not a second too soon.

He peered at the clock. It had the same bloodshot look as the typewriter.

He went into his bathroom, took a shower, and came back in his pyjamas. The first thing he did in his study was to yank the telephone jack out of the wall socket. The second thing he did was to seize Dr. Watson's journal.

It will put me to sleep, he said to himself cunningly.

CHAPTER V

THE DIOGENES CLUB

THE FOLLOWING MORNING I awoke to find Holmes up and pacing. Making no reference whatever to the previous night's misadventure, he said, "Watson, I wonder if you would inscribe a few notes for me?"

"I should be happy to."

"I apologise for demeaning you to the role of amanuensis, but I have a special reason for wishing the details of this case to be put down in orderly fashion."

"A special reason?"

"Very. If your time is free, we shall call this afternoon upon my brother Mycroft, at his club. A consultation may bear us fruit. In certain ways, you know, Mycroft's analytical talents are superior to mine."

"I am aware of the high respect in which you hold him."

"Of course, his is what you might call a sedentary ability, in that he detests moving about. If a street-chair were ever invented to transport one from office to home and back again, Mycroft would be its first purchaser."

"I do recall that he is a man of rigid routine."

"Thus, he tends to reduce all riddles, human or otherwise, to chess-board dimensions. This is far too restrictive for my taste, but his methods are often quite stimulating, in the broader analysis."

Holmes rubbed his hands together. "And now, let us list our actors. Not necessarily in the order of their importance. We have, first, the Duke of Shires..."

Holmes re-capitulated for an hour, whilst I took notes. Then he prowled the rooms whilst I re-arranged my notes into some semblance of order. When I had finished, I handed him the following *résumé*. It contained information of which I had no previous knowledge, data that Holmes had gathered over-night:

The Duke of Shires (Kenneth Osbourne)

Present holder of title and lands dating back to 1420. The twentieth descendant of the line. The Duke lives quietly, dividing his time between his estates and a town-house on Berkeley Square, where he pursues a painter's career. He sired two sons by a wife now ten years deceased. He has never re-married.

Lord Carfax (Richard Osbourne)

Elder son of Kenneth. Lineal inheritor of the duke-dom. He sired one daughter, Deborah. But tragedy struck when his wife perished upon the delivery-table. The child is cared for by a governess at the Devonshire estate. The bond of affection between father and daughter is strong. Lord Carfax exhibits deep humanitarian tendencies. He gives generously of both his money and his time to the Montague Street Hostel in London, a sanctuary for indigents.

Michael Osbourne

Second son of Kenneth. A source of shame and sorrow to his father. Michael, according to testimony, bitterly resented his inferior position as a second son and non-inheritor, and embarked upon a profligate life. Bent, it is said, upon disgracing the title beyond his reach, he is also reported to have married a woman of the streets, apparently for no other reason than to further that misguided end. This reprehensible act is purported to have taken place while he was a medical student in Paris. He was expelled from the Sorbonne shortly thereafter. His fate thenceforward, and his present address, are unknown.

Joseph Beck
A pawn-broker with a shop on Great Heapton Street. Of doubtful importance, on the basis of data at hand.

Dr. Murray
A dedicated M.D. who superintends the Montague Street morgue, and devotes himself to the adjoining hostel he himself created.

Sally Young.
The niece of Dr. Murray. She gives her full-time to the hostel. A devoted nurse and social-worker, it was she who pledged the surgeon's-kit at Beck's pawn-shop. When questioned, she gave information freely, and appeared to hold nothing in reserve.

Pierre
A seemingly harmless imbecile taken in at the hostel, where he performs menial tasks. The surgeon's-case was found among his possessions, and pledged by Miss Young for his benefit. He appears to have come from France.

The Scar-faced Woman
Unidentified.

Holmes ran through the *résumé* with a dissatisfied frown. "If this accomplishes nothing else," said he, "It shows us what a little way we have come, and how far we have still to go. It does not list the victims, who underscore our need for haste. There have been four known butcheries, and any delay on our part will no doubt add to the list. So if you will clothe yourself, Watson, we shall flag a hansom and be off to the Diogenes Club."

Holmes sat deep in thought as we rattled over the cobble-stones, but I risked disturbing him for something that came suddenly to mind.

"Holmes," said I, "as we were leaving the Duke of Shires's estate, you mentioned that Lord Carfax had failed on two counts. I think I have become aware of one of them."

"Indeed?"

"It occurs to me that he made no inquiry as to how you had come by the surgical-case. It therefore seems logical that he already knew."

"Excellent, Watson."

"In the light of the omission, we are justified in assuming that it was he who sent it to you?"

"We have at least a right to suspect that he knows who did."

"Then perhaps Lord Carfax is our key to the identity of the scar-faced woman."

"Entirely possible, Watson. However, recognising a key as such, and turning it, can be two different matters entirely."

"I must confess that his Lordship's second lapse has escaped me."

"You will recall that, in Lord Carfax's presence, I dropped the case and spilled its contents onto the floor? And that he courteously picked up the instruments?"

"Yes?"

"But perhaps you failed to note the practised skill with which he replaced them, each to its proper niche, with no hesitation whatever."

"Why, of course!"

66

"And, now that you recall this, what additional information does it give you concerning his Lordship?"

"That, even though he professes no surgical knowledge or experience, he is quite familiar with the tools of surgery."

"Precisely. A fact that we must place in our mental file for future reference. But here we are, Watson, and Mycroft awaits us."

The Diogenes Club! I remembered it well, even though I had entered its hushed precincts but once. That had been upon the occasion when Mycroft had shifted to his more active brother's shoulders the curious affair of the Greek Interpreter, which case I had the honour and satisfaction of recording for the pleasure of Holmes's not inconsiderable body of admirers.

The Diogenes Club was formed by, and for the benefit of, men who chose to seek solitude in the heart of the clamorous city. It is a luxurious place, with easy-chairs, excellent food, and all the other appurtenances of creature-comfort. The rules are geared to the Club's basic purpose, and are strictly enforced; rules devised to discourage, nay, to forbid, all sociability. Talking, save in the Stranger's Room—into which we were soundlessly ushered—is forbidden. In fact, it is forbidden for any member to take the slightest notice of any other. A tale is told—apocryphal, I am sure—of a member succumbing to a heart-attack in his chair and being found to have expired only when a fellow-member noticed that the *Times* propped before the poor man was three days old.

Mycroft Holmes awaited us in the Stranger's Room, having taken time off, I was later informed, from his government post, around the corner in Whitehall. This, I might add, was an unheard-of interruption of his fixed habits.

Still, neither of the brothers, upon meeting, seemed in

any haste to get to the business at hand. Mycroft, a large, comfortable man with thick grey hair and heavy features, bore little resemblance to his younger brother. He extended his hand, and exclaimed, "Sherlock! You're looking fit. Bouncing all over England and the Continent appears to agree with you." Shifting the meaty hand to me, Mycroft said, "Dr. Watson. I had heard that you escaped from Sherlock's clutch into matrimony. Surely Sherlock has not re-captured you?"

"I am most happily married," I assured him. "My wife is visiting an aunt at the moment."

"And Sherlock's long arm reaches out instantly!"

Mycroft's smile was warm. For an unsocial man, he had a curious talent for making one feel at ease. He had met us at the door, and now he moved towards the bow-window looking out upon one of London's busiest streets. We followed, and the brothers stood side by side, surveying the passing scene.

"Sherlock," said Mycroft, "I have not been in this room since your last visit, but the faces outside never change. From the look of that street, it could have been yesterday."

"Yet," murmured Sherlock, "it has changed. Old intrigues have died, new ones have been born."

Mycroft pointed. "Those two fellows at the kerb. Are they involved in some dire plot?"

"Do you mean the lamp-lighter and the book-keeper?"

"The very men."

"I'd say not. The lamp-lighter is consoling the book-keeper for being recently sacked."

"I agree. The book-keeper will no doubt find a berth, but he will lose it speedily and find himself again on the street."

I was compelled to interrupt. "Come, come," said I, and heard myself repeating my old objections. "This is too much!"

68

"Watson, Watson," chided Mycroft, "after all those years with Sherlock, I should not expect such myopia from you. Even from this distance, surely you observe the smears of ink, both black and red, upon the first man's fingers? Just as surely, the occupational mark of the book-keeper?"

"Observe also," added Holmes the younger, "the ink-blot upon his collar, where he touched pen to linen, and the unpressed condition of his otherwise quite respectable suit."

"From which is it too difficult, my dear Watson," interposed Mycroft, with a kindliness that irritated me, "to project the man's slovenliness to his work, and thus conjure up an irate employer?"

"An employer not only irate but unforgiving," said Sherlock, "as evidenced by the newspaper in the book-keeper's jacket-pocket, opened to the *Situations* column. Hence, he is unemployed."

"But you said he would find a berth!" said I, testily, to Mycroft. "If the fellow is so inefficient, why should a new employer consider him?"

"Most would not, but many of the entries in the newspaper are marked, clearly for investigation. Such energy in seeking a new situation must eventually be rewarded."

I threw up my hands. "I concede, as usual! But the other man's being a lamp-lighter—surely that is sheer surmise on your part?"

"A little more technical," my friend Holmes admitted. "But observe the spot that is worn shiny on his inner right sleeve, extending upwards above the cuff."

"An unfailing mark of the lamp-lighter," said Mycroft.

"In extending his pole to reach the gas-globe with his flame," explained Sherlock, "he rubs the lower end of the pole against that portion of his sleeve again and again. Really elementary, Watson."

Before I could retort, Holmes's mood changed, and he turned from the window with a frown. "I wish our present problem were as easily solved. That is why we are here, Mycroft."

"Give me the details," replied his brother, with a smile. "My afternoon must not be entirely lost."

Twenty minutes later, ensconced in easy-chairs in the Stranger's Room, we sat in silence. It was broken by Mycroft. "Your picture is well-delineated, Sherlock, so far as it goes. But surely you are capable of solving the riddle yourself."

"I have no doubt of that, but there is little time. Preventing further outrages is urgent. Two minds are better than one. You might well discern a point that would save me a precious day or two of searching."

"Then let us see precisely what you have. Or, rather, precisely what you do not have. Your pieces are far from complete."

"Of course."

"Yet you have touched a sensitive spot somewhere, as witness the swift and murderous attack upon you and Watson. Unless you wish to ascribe it to coincidence?"

"I do not!"

"Nor I." Mycroft tugged at an ear. "Of course, it is no cerebral feat to identify the mysterious Pierre by his true name."

"Certainly not," replied Holmes. "He is the Duke of Shires's second son, Michael."

"As to Michael's grievous injuries, the father may be unaware of them. But Lord Carfax certainly knows of Michael's presence at the hostel, and beyond doubt recognised his younger brother."

"I am quite aware," said Holmes, "that Lord Carfax has not been entirely candid."

"He interests me. The philanthropic cloak is an admirable disguise for devilry. Lord Carfax could well have been responsible for Michael's delivery into Dr. Murray's care."

"Also," said Holmes, grimly, "for his injuries."

"Possibly. But you must find other pieces, Sherlock."

"Time, Mycroft, time! That is my problem. I must identify, quickly, the right thread in this skein, and seize upon it."

"I think you must somehow force Carfax's hand."

I broke in. "May I ask a question?"

"By all means, Watson. We had no intention of excluding you."

"I can be of little help, but certainly identifying Jack the Ripper is our first concern. Therefore I ask, do you believe we have met the murderer? Is the Ripper one of the people with whom we have come in contact?"

Sherlock Holmes smiled. "Do you have a candidate for that dubious honour, Watson?"

"If I were compelled to make a selection, I should name the imbecile. But I must confess that I missed badly in not postulating him as Michael Osbourne."

"On which grounds do you condemn him?"

"Nothing tangible, I fear. But I cannot forget the *tableau* I witnessed as we were leaving the Montague Street morgue. Dr. Murray, you will recall, commanded 'Pierre' to cover the unfortunate's corpse. There was nothing conclusive in his action, but his manner made my flesh fairly crawl. He seemed entranced by the mutilated cadaver. In smoothing out the sheet, his hands ran lovingly over the cold flesh. He appeared to be enamoured of the butchery."

There was a pause during which the brothers evaluated my contribution. Then Mycroft said, gravely, "You have made a most pertinent point, Watson. I would only say that it is difficult, as you are aware, to interpret the actions generated by a damaged mentality. However, your instinc-

71

tive revulsion may be worth more than all the logic we can muster."

"The observation is certainly to be considered," remarked Sherlock.

I gathered the impression, however, that neither put any great stock in my statement; that they were merely being kind.

Mycroft came ponderously to his feet. "You must gather more facts, Sherlock."

His brother clenched his hands.

It had occurred to me that this entire episode with Mycroft was not at all like the sure-footed, self-confident Sherlock Holmes I had known. I was puzzling the matter when Mycroft, speaking quietly, said, "I believe I know the source of your confusion, Sherlock. You must banish it. You have become subjective in regard to this case."

"I fail to comprehend," Holmes said, a trifle coldly.

"Four of the most heinous murders of the century, and perhaps more to come. If you had entered the case sooner, you might have prevented some of these. That is what gnaws at you. The acid of guilt can dull the keenest intellect."

Holmes had no rebuttal. He shook his head impatiently, and said, "Come, Watson, the game is afoot. We stalk a savage beast."

"And a cunning one," said Mycroft, in clear warning. Then he said, "Sherlock, you seek a scar-faced woman. Also, one of the key-pieces that is missing, the ill-reputed wife of Michael Osbourne. What does that suggest?"

Holmes fixed his brother with an angry eye. "You must indeed feel that I have lost my faculties, Mycroft! It of course suggests that they are one and the same."

On that note, we left the Diogenes Club.

Ellery Nemesis Investigates

THE APARTMENT bell was a carved rosebud set in ivory leaves. Grant Ames jabbed it, and the result was a girl wearing poisonous-green lounging pyjamas.

"Hello, Madge. I happened to be in the neighborhood, so here I am."

She glowed. That thinly patrician male face reminded her of a very big dollar sign. "And so you thought you'd drop in?" she said, making it sound like Einstein's first formulation of the Theory; and she threw the door so wide it cracked against the wall.

Grant moved warily forward. "Nice little nest you've got here."

"It's just an ordinary career gal's efficiency apartment. I combed the East side, absolutely combed it. And finally found this. It's sickeningly expensive, but of course one wouldn't dare live anywhere but Upper East."

"I didn't know you'd gone in for a career."

"Oh, definitely. I'm a consultant. You drink scotch, don't you?"

It behoved a legman to follow through, Grant thought. He asked brightly, "And with whom do you consult?"

"The public relations people at the factory."

"The one your father owns, of course."

"Of course."

Madge Short was a daughter of Short's Shapely Shoes, but with three brothers and two sisters to share the eventual loot. She wagged her pert red head as she extended a scotch-and.

"And the factory is located—"

"In Iowa."

"You commute?"

"Silly! There's a Park Avenue office."

"You surprise me, dear heart. I see you in a different role."

"As a bride?" Two outstanding young breasts lifted the poisonous green like votive offerings.

"God, no," Grant said hurriedly. "I visualize you somewhere in the literary field."

"You've got to be kidding!"

Grant had checked the room. There were no books in sight—no magazines, either—but that wasn't necessarily conclusive.

"I see you as reading a great deal, chickie. A bit of a bookworm, so to speak."

"In this day and age? Wherever would one get the *time?*"

"Oh, one wedges it in here and there."

"I do read some. *Sex and the Single—*"

"I'm a detective bug myself. Father Brown. Bishop Cushing." He watched narrowly for her reaction. It was like watching for a pink piglet to react.

"I like them, too."

"With a smattering," Grant went on cunningly, "of the philosophers—Burton, Sherlock Holmes."

"One of the men at that party, he's an expert on Zen." Doubt was beginning to creep in. Grant quickly changed his tactics.

"That blue bikini you wore. Was it ever sharp?"

"I'm so glad you liked it, dahling. How about another scotch?"

"No, thanks," Grant said, getting up. "Time goes

bucketing by, and—well, there you are." She was hopeless.

He collapsed behind the wheel of the Jag.

How did those fellows do it? Holmes? Even Queen?

While something was pressing against Ellery's nose, smothering him. He awoke and discovered that it was the journal with which he had gone to bed. He yawned, dropped it on the floor, and sat up groggily, elbows on knees. The journal now lay between his feet, so he doubled up, head between his hands.

And began to read, southward.

CHAPTER VI

I STALK THE RIPPER

THE FOLLOWING MORNING, I must say, Holmes infuriated me.

When I awoke, he was up and clothed. I instantly saw, from the reddened condition of his eyes, that he had slept little; indeed, I suspected that he had been out all night. But I made no inquiry.

To my gratification, he was of a mind to talk, rather than to sink into one of his reticent moods, out of which little more than cryptic sounds ever emerged.

"Watson," said he, without preliminary, "there is a notorious public-house in Whitechapel."

"There are many."

"True, but the one to which I refer, The Angel and Crown, abuses even the riotous pleasures tendered by that district. It is situated in the heart of the Ripper's prowling-grounds, and three of the murdered prostitutes were seen on the premises shortly before their deaths. I mean to give sharp attention to The Angel and Crown. To-night I shall indulge in a little carousing there."

"Capital, Holmes! If I may confine myself to ale—"

"Not you, my dear Watson. I still shudder at how close to death I have already led you."

"See here, Holmes—"

"My mind is made up," replied he, firmly. "I have no intention of confronting your good wife, upon her return, with the dismal news that her husband's body may be found in the morgue."

"I thought I gave a good account of myself!" said I, heatedly.

"You did, certainly. Without you I might myself well be occupying a pallet in Dr. Murray's establishment. That is no justification, however, for risking your safety a second time. Perhaps whilst I am absent to-day—I have much to do—your practice could do with a little attention."

"It is going along quite nicely, thank you. I have a working arrangement with a most able locum tenens."

"Then might I suggest a concert, or a good book?"

"I am quite capable of occupying my mind fruitfully," said I, coldly.

"Indeed you are, Watson," said he. "Well, I must be off! Expect me when you see me. I promise I shall put you abreast of affairs upon my return."

With that he darted out, leaving me to steam at a temperature only a little below that of Mrs. Hudson's tea.

My determination to defy Holmes did not form at once; but, before my morning repast was finished, it was clearly shaped. I passed the day reading a curious monograph from Holmes's book-shelf on the possible use of bees in murder-intrigues, both by causing them to contaminate their honey, and by training them to attack a victim in a swarm. The work was anonymous, but I recognised the concise style of Holmes in the writing. Then, as darkness fell, I planned my night's foray.

I would arrive at The Angel and Crown in the guise of a lecherous man-about-town, sure that I would not stand out, as many of London's more hardened *habitués* made a practise of frequenting such places. I therefore hurried home and donned evening attire. Capping my regalia with top-hat and opera cape, I surveyed myself in the glass, and found that I cut a more dashing figure than I had dared hope. Slipping a loaded revolver into my pocket, I went out

77

into the street, hailed a hansom, and gave The Angel and Crown as my destination.

Holmes had not yet arrived.

It was a horrible place. The long, low-ceilinged public-room was thick with eye-smarting fumes from the many oil-lamps. Clouds of tobacco smoke hung in the air, like storm-warnings. And the crude tables were crowded by as motley a collection of humanity as ever I had encountered. Evil-faced Lascars on leave from the freighters that choke the Thames; inscrutable Orientals; Swedes, and Africans, and seedy-looking Europeans; not to mention the many varieties of native Britons—all bent on supping off the flesh-pots of the world's largest city.

The flesh-pots were dubiously spiced with females of all ages and conditions. Most were pitiful in their physical deterioration. Only a few were attractive, younger ones who had just set foot upon the downward path.

It was one of these latter who approached me after I had found a table, had ordered a pint of stout, and sat surveying the reckless scene. She was a pretty little thing, but the wicked light in her eye, and her hard manner, indelibly marked her.

" 'Ullo, luv. Buy a gel a gin-an'-bitters?"

I was about to decline the honour, but a brutish-looking waiter standing by cried, "Gin-an'-bitters for the lady!" and ploughed towards the bar. The man was no doubt paid on the basis of the liquor the girls wheedled from their marks.

The wench dropped into the chair opposite me and laid her rather dirty hand upon mine. I withdrew mine quickly. This brought an uncertain smile to her painted lips, but her voice was cajoling as she said, "Shy, ducks? No need to be."

"I merely dropped in for a quick pint," said I. The adventure no longer seemed so alluring.

"Sure, luv. All the toffs drop in for quick pints. Then they just 'appen to find out what else we 'ave for sale."

The waiter returned, slopped down the gin-and-tonic, and fumbled among the coins I had laid upon the table. I was sure he appropriated several pence too many, but I did not make an issue of it.

"Me name's Polly, luv. What's yers?"

"Hawkins," said I, quickly. "Sam Hawkins."

"'Awkins, is it?" she laughed. "Well, it's a bit of a change from Smythe. Yer 'eart'd bleed at 'ow many bloody Smythes come 'round."

My reply, if indeed I had any, was cut down by an outburst in another part of the room. A dark-visaged sailor of gorilla proportions gave out a roar of rage and upset a table in his zeal to get at another patron who appeared to have offended him, a Chinese of insignificant stature. For a moment it seemed likely that the Oriental would be killed, so ferocious was the sailor's aspect.

But then another man interposed himself. He was thick-browed, with a heavy neck, and shoulders and arms like trees, although he did not match the angry sailor's proportions. The Oriental's unexpected defender smashed his fist into the sailor's solar plexus. It was a mighty blow, and the sailor's grasp could be heard all over the room as he doubled over in agony. Again the smaller man measured the giant, and again he delivered a blow, this time to the brute's jaw. The sailor's head snapped back; his eyes glazed; and, as he collapsed, his assailant was ready with a hunched shoulder, and caught the man's body like a sack of meal. His load balanced, the victor made calmly for the door, lugging the unconscious mariner as though he weighed no more than a child. He opened the door and hurled the man into the street.

"That's Max Klein," said my doxy in awe. "Strong as a

bloody ox, 'e is. Max just bought this place. 'E's owned it for about a four-month, an' 'e don't allow no bloke to get killed in it, 'e don't."

The performance had been impressive indeed; but, at that moment, something else drew my attention. The door through which Klein had flung the sailor had scarcely closed when it was put to use by a new customer, one whom I thought I recognised. I peered through the haze to make sure my identification was correct. There was no doubt. It was Joseph Beck, the pawnbroker, moving towards a table. I made a mental note to report this fact to Holmes, and then I turned back to Polly.

"I got a nice room, luv," said she, in a seductive tone.

"I fear I'm not interested, Madam," said I, as kindly as I could.

"Madame, 'e says!" cried she, with indignation. "I ain't *that* old, guv'ner. I'm young enough, I promise yer. Young *an'* clean. You 'ave nothin' to fear from me."

"But there must be someone *you* fear, Polly," said I, observing her closely.

"Me? I don't go ter 'urt nobody."

"I mean the Ripper."

A whining note leaped into her voice. "Yer just tryin' to scare me! Well, I ain't afraid." She took a gulp of her drink, eyes darting here and there. They came to focus on a point over my shoulder, and I realised that they had been directed that way during most of our conversation. I turned my head, and beheld as vicious-looking a creature as the imagination could have conjured.

He was incredibly filthy, and he had a hideous knife-scar across one cheek. This twisted his mouth in a permanent leer, and the damaged flesh around his left eye added further to his frightful aspect. I have never seen such malevolence in a human face.

"'E got Annie, the Ripper did," Polly whispered. "'E

gouged the poor little thing up good—Annie wot never 'urt a soul."

I turned back to her. "That brute there, with the knife-scar?"

"'Oo knows?" Then she cried, "Wot's he 'ave to go and do those things for? Wot's the fun in shovin' a blade into a poor gel's belly an' cuttin' off 'er breast an' all?"

He was the man.

Explaining my absolute certainty is difficult. In earlier life I indulged for a time in gambling, as a young man will, and there is a feeling that comes over one on certain occasions that is not founded in reason. Instinct, a sixth sense—call it what you will—it comes, and it is impossible to ignore it.

Such a feeling came over me as I studied the creature behind us; his gaze was fixed upon the girl who sat with me, and I could see the foul slaver at the corners of his contorted mouth.

But what to do?

"Polly," I asked, quietly, "did you ever see that man before?"

"Me, ducks? Not ever! Narsty-lookin' cove, ain't 'e?" Then, with the instability that characterises the loose woman, Polly's mood changed. Her natural recklessness, possibly re-inforced by too many drinks, came to the fore. She suddenly raised her glass.

"'Ere's luck, luv. If yer don't want me lily-white body, yer don't. But yer a good bloke, and I wish yer the best."

"Thank you."

"A gel's got t'make a livin', so I'll be off. Another night, maybe?"

"Perhaps."

She arose from the table, and moved away, flaunting her hips, I watched her, anticipating that she would approach another table for another solicitation. But she did

81

not. Instead, she scanned the room, and then moved swiftly towards the door. She had found the pickings poor that night in The Angel and Crown, I thought and was going to resort to the streets. I had scarcely begun to feel relief when the repulsive creature beyond my shoulder jumped up and set out after her. My alarm may be imagined. I could think of no other course than to touch the weapon in my pocket for reassurance, and follow the man to the street.

I was beset by a momentary blindness, having to adjust my eyesight to the darkness after the glare of the public-room. When my eyes focused, fortunately, the man was still within my view. He was skulking along, close by the wall, at the end of the street.

I was now certain that I was embarked upon a perilous course. He was the Ripper. and he was stalking the girl who had endeavoured to entice me to her room, and there was only I between her and a hideous death. I gripped my revolver convulsively.

I followed, treading on the balls of my feet like a Red Indian of the American plains. He turned the corner; and, fearful both of losing him and of finding him, I hurried after.

I rounded the corner, panting, and peered cautiously ahead. There was only one gas-lamp, which made my survey doubly difficult. I strained my eyes. But my quarry had disappeared.

Apprehension seized me. Perhaps the fiend had already dragged the poor girl into an areaway and was slashing the life from her young body. If only I had had the foresight to bring a pocket lantern! I ran forward into darkness, the profound silence of the street broken only by the sounds of my footsteps.

There was enough light to warn me that the street narrowed at the other end, coming down to a passageway.

It was into this that I plunged, my heart in my mouth at what I might find.

Suddenly I heard a choked cry. I had collided with something soft. A fear-stricken voice babbled, "Mercy! Oh, pray 'ave mercy!"

It was Polly, who had been pressed against the wall in the darkness. In fear that her cries might frighten the Ripper away, I clapped my hand over her mouth and whispered into her ear.

"It's all right, Polly. You are in no danger. I am the gentleman you sat with. I followed you—"

I was struck from behind by a sudden, enormous weight, and knocked back, staggering, along the passage. But my brain still functioned. I had been outwitted by the cunning devil I had followed from The Angel and Crown. He had crept into some shadow and allowed me to pass him. Now, enraged at the prospect of being deprived of his prey, he was attacking like a jungle beast.

I answered in kind, fighting desperately, trying to pull the revolver from my pocket. It should have been in my hand; but, during my stint in her Majesty's Indian service, I had served as a surgeon, not a soldier; I had no training in hand-to-hand fighting.

I was therefore no match for the monster with whom I had come to grips. I went down under his onslaught, gratefully aware that the girl had fled. I felt his powerful hands on my throat, and I flailed out desperately with my free arm as I struggled still to clear the weapon from my pocket.

To my stupefaction, a familiar voice growled, "Now let us see what manner of beast I have flushed!" Even before a bull's lantern flashed, I became aware of my blunder. The evil-appearing creature seated behind me in the pub had been Holmes—in disguise!

"Watson!" He was as astonished as I.

83

"Holmes! Good heavens, man! Had I managed to get my revolver out, I might have shot you!"

"And a good thing, too," grumbled he. "Watson, you can write me down an ass." He lifted his lithe body from me and grasped my hand to help me to my feet. Even then knowing he was my old friend, I could only marvel at the cleverness of his disguise, so different did he appear.

We had no time for further recriminations. As Holmes was pulling me erect, a scream rent the night. His hand released me instantly, and down I tumbled again. An oath erupted from his throat, one of the very few outbursts of profanity I have ever heard from him.

"I've been outdone!" he cried; and he went streaking away into the night.

As I scrambled to my feet, the female cries of terror and pain increased in volume. Suddenly they were cut off; and the sounds of a second pair of running feet were added to those of Holmes.

I must confess that I showed to little advantage in the affair. I had once been the middle-weight boxing champion of my regiment, but those days were in the long-ago, and I leaned against the brick wall, fighting nausea and dizziness. At that moment, I should not have been able to respond had our gracious Queen herself been screaming for aid.

The vertigo passed; the world righted itself; I moved shakily back, as I had come, groping my way along through the silence that had ominously fallen. I had retraced my steps some two hundred paces, when a quiet voice stopped me.

"Here, Watson."

"I turned to my left and discovered a break in the wall. Again, Holmes's voice: "I dropped my lantern. Will you be so kind as to search for it, Watson?"

His quiet tone was doubly chilling, in that it concealed

an agonised inner struggle. I knew Holmes; he was shaken to the core.

Good fortune attended my search for the lantern. I took a single step, and bumped it with my foot. I relighted it, and staggered back from one of the most horrible scenes that has ever met my eyes.

Holmes was on his knees, back bowed, head lowered, a picture of despair.

"I have failed, Watson. I should be brought to the dock for criminal stupidity."

I scarcely heard him, stunned as I was by the bloody sight that confronted me. Jack the Ripper had vented his obscene madness upon poor Polly. Her clothing had been torn from her body, baring fully half of it to view. A great, ragged slash had opened her abdomen, and its torn and mutilated contents were exposed like those of a butchered animal. A second savage thrust had severed her left breast almost from her body. The terrible scene swam before my eyes.

"But he had so little time! How—?"

But Holmes came alive; he sprang to his feet. "Come Watson! Follow me!"

So abruptly did he launch himself from the areaway towards the street that I was left behind. I called upon the reserves of strength each man possesses in moments of emergency, and ran, pell-mell, after him. He was well in the forefront all the way, but I did not lose him; and, when I again came close, I found him thundering upon the door of Joseph Beck's pawn-shop.

"Beck!" Holmes shouted. "Come out! I demand that you come out this instant!" His fists smote again and again upon the panel. "Open this door, or I shall smash it in!"

A rectangle of light appeared overhead. A window opened; a head was thrust out. Joseph Beck cried, "Are you mad? Who are you?"

The light from the lamp in his hand revealed a red-tasselled night-cap and a high-necked night-dress.

Holmes stood back and bellowed up at him. "Sir, I am Sherlock Holmes, and if you do not come down immediately I shall climb this wall and drag you out by your hair!"

Beck was, understandably, shaken. Holmes was still in his disguise; and to be roused out of sleep, and find such a hideous figure banging at his door in the dead of night, was certainly not an experience for which the life of a tradesman had prepared the pawnbroker.

I sought to help. "Herr Breck! You remember me, do you not?"

He gaped down at me. "You are one of the two gentlemen—?"

"And, despite his appearance, this is the other, Mr Sherlock Holmes, I promise you."

The pawnbroker hesitated; but then he said, "Very well; I shall come down."

Holmes paced with impatient strides until the light appeared in the shop, and the street-door opened.

"Step out here, Beck!" commanded Holmes, in a deadly voice; and, fearfully, the German obeyed. My friend's powerful hand darted out, and the man shrank back, but he was too slow. Holmes tore open the front of his night-dress, revealing a bare chest pimpled with the chill.

"What are you doing, sir?" quavered the tradesman. "I do not understand."

"Be silent!" said Holmes, harshly; and in the light of Beck's lamp he examined the pawn-broker's chest minutely. "Where did you go, Joseph Beck, after you left the Angel and Crown?" asked Holmes, releasing his grasp.

"Where did I go? I came home to bed!" Reassured by Holmes's milder tone, Beck was now hostile.

"Yes," replied Holmes thoughtfully, "it appears that

you did. Go back to bed, sir. I am sorry if I have frightened you."

With this, Holmes turned unceremoniously away, and I followed. I looked back as we reached the corner, to see Herr Beck still standing before his shop. Holding the lamp high above his head, he appeared for all the world like a night-shirted caricature of that noble statue, Liberty Enlightening the World, presented to the United States by the people of France, the great, hollow, bronze figure that now stands in the harbour at New York City.

We returned to the scene of the butchery, to find that the body of poor Polly had been discovered. An army of the morbidly curious choked the entrance to the street, whilst the lanterns of officialdom illuminated the darkness beyond.

Holmes gazed grimly at the scene, hands thrust deep into his pockets. "There is no point in identifying ourselves, Watson," said he, in a mutter. "It would only make for profitless conversation with Lestrade."

It did not surprise me that Holmes preferred not to reveal our part in that night's terrible affair. It was not merely that he had his methods; in this circumstance, his self-esteem was involved, and it had suffered a grievous blow.

"Let's slip away, Watson," said he, bitterly, "like the addle-brained idiots we have become."

CHAPTER VII

THE SLAYER OF HOGS

"What you failed to see, Watson, was the cloaked figure of Joseph Beck leaving the pub, just as the girl gave evidence of her intention to go elsewhere. You had eyes only for me."

It was dismally evident to me that I had been the culprit, not he, but there was no hint of this in his voice. I attempted to assess the blame, but he cut short my apologies. "No, no," said he, "it was my stupidity that let the monster slip through our fingers, not yours."

Chin on breast, Holmes went on. "When I emerged from the pub, the girl was just turning the corner. Beck was nowhere in sight, and I could only assume either that he had made off in the other direction, or was crouched in one of the dark doorways nearby. I chose the latter assumption. I followed the girl around the corner and heard approaching footsteps, catching a glimpse of a caped man entering behind us. Not dreaming that it was you— your figure and Beck's do not greatly differ, I fear, Watson—I took the skulker to be our pawnbroker. I hid myself in turn, and you passed me. Then I heard the cries, and I thought I had stalked the Ripper successfully. Whereupon I attacked, and discovered my unforgiveable error."

We had finished our morning tea, and Holmes was pacing his quarters at Baker Street in a fury. I followed his movements sadly, wishing I possessed the power to erase the whole incident from the slate, not only for Polly's sake, but for my friend's peace of mind.

"Then," continued Holmes, savagely, "whilst we were preoccupied with our blunders, the Ripper struck. The arrogance of this fiend!" cried he. "The contempt, the utter self-confidence, with which he perpetrates his outrages! Believe me, Watson, I shall lay the monster by the heels if it is the last act of my life!"

"It would appear," said I, trying to divert his bitter thoughts, "that Joseph Beck has been exonerated, at least of last night's murder."

"Quite so. Beck could not possibly have reached his quarters, cleansed himself of the blood, undressed, and donned night-clothes before we were upon him." Holmes seized his cherry-wood, and his Persian slipper, then cast them down in disgust. "Watson," said he, "all we accomplished last night was to eliminate one suspect from amongst London's millions. At such a rate, we shall succeed in spotting our quarry some time during the next century!"

I could find nothing to say in refutation. But then Holmes suddenly threw back his spare shoulders and directed a steely glance at me. "But enough of this, Watson! We shall imitate the Phoenix. Get dressed. We are going to pay another visit to Dr. Murray's mortuary."

Within the hour, we stood before the Montague Street portal to that gloomy establishment. Holmes glanced up and down the shabby thoroughfare.

"Watson," said he, "I should like a more detailed picture of this neighbourhood. Whilst I venture inside, will you be good enough to scout the near streets?"

Eager to atone for my bungling of the previous night, I readily agreed.

"When you have finished, you will no doubt find me in the hostel." Holmes disappeared through the morgue gate.

I found that the vicinity of Montague Street possessed

no common commercial establishments. The further side was occupied by a row of warehouses that presented locked entrances and no signs of life.

But when I turned the corner, I came upon a more active scene. I saw a green-grocer's stall, where a house-wife haggled with the proprietor over the price of a cabbage. The shop next door housed a tobacconist's. Just beyond, there stood a small, evil-looking public-house with a weathered replica of a hansom cab above the door.

My attention was soon drawn to an open entranceway on the street's near side. A great squealing emanated therefrom. It sounded as if a battalion of pigs was being slaughtered. As it turned out, this was precisely the case. I entered through an ancient stone archway, came out into a courtyard, and found myself in an abattoir. Four lean, live hogs were penned in one corner; the butcher, a grossly-muscled youth in a bloody leather apron, was in the act of dragging a fifth towards a suspended hook. In a callous manner, he hoisted the animal, and chained its hind legs to the hook. A rusted pulley creaked as he hauled on the rope. He tied a swift knot, and the hog squealed and thrashed as if it knew its fate.

As I watched in disgust, the butcher's boy took up a long knife and, without a qualm, plunged it into the hog's throat. The sounds gurgled away, and the boy stepped back to avoid the gout of dark blood. Then, he walked carelessly into the red pool, and slashed the animal's throat open. Whereupon the knife swept down, opening the animal from tail to jowls.

It was not the butchery, however, that made me look away. My glance was drawn to what appeared to me even more horrible—the sight of the idiot, the creature whom both Sherlock Holmes and his brother Mycroft had identified as Michael Osbourne. He was crouched in one corner of the abattoir, oblivious of all else but the butcher's work. The operation seemed to fascinate him. His eyes drank in the bloody carcase of the animal in a manner that I can only describe as obscene.

His preliminary work done, the butcher's boy stepped back and favoured me with a smile.

"Lookin' for a bit o' pork, guv'ner?"

"No, thank you! I was strolling by—"

"An' you heard the squealin'. Yer has to be a stranger, guv'ner, else you would not o' bothered. The neighbourhood's used to their ruddy noise." He turned cheerfully to Michael Osbourne. "Ain't that right, dummy?"

The imbecile smiled and nodded.

"The dummy's the on'y one that keeps me comp'ny. I'd be fair lonesome 'thout him."

"Your work is certainly not carried on under the most cleanly conditions," said I, distastefully.

"Clean-ly, says 'e," chuckled the boy. "Guv'ner, folk 'ereabouts 've got a fat lot more to turn their stomachs than a little dirt on their pork—bloody right they 'ave!" He winked. "The gels, 'specially. They're too busy o' nights keepin' their own 'ides in one piece."

"You refer to the Ripper?"

"That I do, guv, that I do. 'E's keepin' the tarts nervy o' late."

"Did you know the girl who was murdered last night?"

"I did. Passed 'er two-and-six t'other night for a quick whack, I did. Poor little tart didn't 'ave 'er rent, and I'm that gen'rous, I 'ates to see a gel trampin' the ruddy streets in the fog fer want o' a bed."

Some instinct made me pursue the tasteless conversation. "Have you any idea as to the identity of the Ripper?"

"Lord love yer, guv. 'E might just be yer own lordship, now, mightn't 'e? Yer got to admit, 'e's prob'ly a toff, don't yer?"

"Why do you say that?"

"Well, now, let's look at it this way. I'm at 'ome with blood in my perfession, cozy with it, yer might say, and so I 'ave to think that way, right?"

"What are you driving at?"

"Guv, the way that Ripper carves 'em up, 'e's just got to get smeary. But nobody's never seen a smeared-up bloke runnin' from one o' those murders, now, 'ave they?"

"I believe not," said I, rather startled.

"An' why not, guv'ner? 'Cause a toff wearin' a opry cloak over 'is duds could cover up the bloody res-ee-doo, so ter speak! Wouldn't yer say? Well, I 'ave ter get back to this carcase."

I fled the stench and gore of the place. But I took an image with me, that of Michael Osbourne squatting in his corner, laving the slaughter with watering eyes. No matter what Holmes had said, the misshapen wreck of humanity remained my principal suspect.

I circumnavigated the square and made my entrance into the morgue through the Montague Street gate, the adjacent premises fixed in mind. The morgue was untenanted, save for the dead. Traversing its narrow length, I paused near the raised table that was reserved for unwilling guests. A white-sheeted form lay there. I contemplated it for a few moments; then, moved by pity, I drew the sheet back from the face.

Her sufferings past, Polly's marble features reflected acceptance of whatever she had found beyond the pale. I do not rate myself a sentimental man, but I do believe that there is a dignity in death, however it comes. Nor am I deeply religious. Still, I breathed a small prayer for the salvation of this unhappy child's spirit. Then I went away.

I found Holmes in the dining-hall of the hostel, in company with Lord Carfax and Miss Sally Young. The latter gave me a smile of welcome. "Dr. Watson, may I fetch you a cup of tea?"

I declined with thanks, and Holmes spoke crisply. "You arrive fortuitously, Watson. Lord Carfax is about to tender some information." His Lordship looked a trifle dubious. "You may speak before my colleague in complete confidence, your Lordship."

"Very well. I was about to relate, Mr. Holmes, Michael left London for Paris some two years ago. I expected him to live a licentious life in that most licentious of cities, but I strove to keep in touch with him, nonetheless; and I was both surprised and gratified to learn that he had entered the Sorbonne to study medicine. We maintained a correspondence, and I became optimistic as to his future. He appeared to have turned a new leaf." At this point, his Lordship's eyes lowered, and a great sadness came over his sensitive face. "But then, disaster struck. I was stunned to learn that Michael had married a woman of the streets."

"Did you meet her, my lord?"

"Never, Mr. Holmes! I frankly admit that I had little stomach for a face-to-face encounter. It is true, however, that I would have confronted the woman, had the opportunity arisen."

"How, then, do you know she was a prostitute? Your brother would hardly have included such an item in his bill of particulars when he informed you of his marriage."

"My brother did not inform me. I received the information in a letter from one of his fellow-students, a person I had never met, but whose written word reflected an earnest interest in Michael's welfare. This gentleman acquainted me with Angela Osbourne's calling, and suggested that, if I had my brother's future at heart, I should

93

leave for Paris immediately and try to repair his fortunes before they were irretrievably destroyed.'"

"You informed your father of this communication?"

"Indeed I did not!" said Lord Carfax, sharply. "Unhappily, my correspondent saw to that. He had dispatched two letters, in the event one should be ignored, I suppose."

"How did your father react?"

"You need hardly ask that question, Mr. Holmes."

"The Duke did not reserve judgement until proof was forthcoming?"

"He did not. The letter was too patently truthful; I did not doubt it myself. As for my father, it was in perfect consonance with what he had always expected of Michael." Lord Carfax paused, pain invading his face. "I shall not soon forget the renunciation. I suspected that Father had also received a letter, and I rushed to his town-house. He was at his easel when I arrived; as I entered the studio, his model drew a robe over her nudity, and my father laid down his brush and surveyed me calmly. He said, 'Richard, what brings you here at this time of day?'

"I saw the tell-tale envelope with the French stamp lying by his palette, and I pointed to it. 'That, your Grace. I presume it is from Paris.'

"'You are correct.' He picked up the envelope, but did not remove its contents. 'It is inappropriate. It should have been edged in black.'

"'I do not understand you,' I replied.

"He laid the letter down, coldly. 'Should not all announcements of death be thus marked? So far as I am concerned, Richard, this letter informs me of Michael's demise. In my heart, the service has already been read, and the body is in the earth.'

"His terrible words stunned me. But, knowing that argument was futile, I left."

"You made no effort to reach Michael?" asked Holmes.

"I did not, sir. To me, he was beyond salvation. Some months later, however, I received an anonymous note, saying that I would find something of interest if I made a visit to this hostel. I did so. I do not have to tell you what I found."

"The note. Did you preserve it, your Lordship?"

"No."

"A pity."

Lord Carfax appeared to be struggling with a natural reticence. Finally, he burst out, "Mr. Holmes, I cannot express to you my shock at finding Michael in his present condition, the victim of an attack so savage that it had turned him into what you have seen—a misshapen creature with but the merest fragment of his reason left."

"How did you proceed, if I may ask?"

Lord Carfax shrugged his shoulders. "The hostel seemed as good a place as any for him. So that part of the problem was solved."

Miss Sally Young had been sitting in amazed silence, her eyes never leaving his Lordship's face. Lord Carfax took cognizance of this. With a sad smile, he said, "I trust you will forgive me, my dear, for not setting the case before you earlier. But it seemed unnecessary—indeed imprudent. I wished Michael to remain here; and, in truth, I was not eager to confess his identity to you and your uncle."

"I understand," said the girl, quietly. "You were entitled to keep your secret my lord, if for no other reason than your support of the hostel has been so generous."

The nobleman seemed embarrassed. "I should have contributed to the maintenance of the hostel in any event, my dear. However, I do not deny that Michael's refuge here enhanced my interest. So perhaps my motives have been as selfish as they have been eleemosynary."

Holmes had been studying Lord Carfax keenly as the story unfolded.

"You made no further efforts in your brother's behalf?"

"One," replied his Lordship. "I communicated with the Paris police, as well as with Scotland Yard, inquiring if their records bore any report of an attack such as my brother had suffered. Their records did not reveal one."

"So you left it there?"

"Yes!" cried the harassed nobleman. "And why not?"

"The felons might have been brought to justice."

"By what method? Michael had become a hopeless idiot. I doubt if he would have been able to recognise his assailants. Even could he have done so, his testimony in a criminal proceeding would have been valueless."

"I see," said Holmes, gravely; but I perceived that he was far from satisfied. "And as to his wife, Angela Osbourne?"

"I never found her."

"Did you not suspect that she wrote the anonymous note?"

"I assumed that she did."

Holmes came to his feet. "I wish to thank your Lordship for being so candid under the difficult circumstances."

This brought a bleak smile. "I assure you, sir, that it has not been through choice. I have no doubt that you would have come by the information through other channels. Now, perhaps, you can let the matter rest."

"Hardly, I fear."

Lord Carfax's face became intense. "I tell you, upon my honour, sir, that Michael has had nothing to do with the horrible murders that have convulsed London!"

"You reassure me," replied Holmes, "and I promise your

Lordship that I will do my utmost to spare you further suffering."

Lord Carfax bowed, and said nothing more.

With that, we took our leave. But as we went out of the hostel, I could see only Michael Osbourne, crouched in that filthy abattoir, enchanted by the blood.

Ellery's Legman Reports

GRANT AMES III lay on Ellery's sofa balancing the glass on his chest, exhausted. "I went forth an eager beaver. I return a wreck."

"From only two interviews?"

"A party is one thing—you can escape behind a patio plant. But alone, trapped inside four walls..."

Ellery, still in pyjamas, crouched over his typewriter and scratched the foundations of a magnificent beard. He typed four more words and stopped.

"The interviews bore no fruit?"

"Two gardensful, one decked in spring green, the other in autumnal purple. But with price tags on the goodies."

"Marriage might be your salvation."

The idler shuddered, "If masochism is one of your vices, old buddy, we'll discuss it. But later, when I get my strength back."

"You're sure neither put the journal in your car?"

"Madge Short thinks Sherlock is some kind of new hair-do. And Katherine Lambert—Kat's not a bad kitten from the neck down. She paints, you know. Redid a loft in the Village. Very intense. The coiled-spring type. You sit there waiting to get the broken end in your eye."

"They may have put you on," Ellery said brutally. "You wouldn't be hard to fool."

"I satisfied myself," Grant said with dignity. "I asked subtle questions. Deep. Searching."

"Such as?"

"Such as, 'Kat, did you put a manuscript addressed to Ellery Queen into the seat of my car at Lita's bash the other day?'"

"And she replied?"

Grant shrugged. "It came in the form of a counter-question—'Who's Ellery Queen?'"

"Have I asked you to leave lately?"

"Let's be kind to each other, friend." Grant paused to drink deeply. "I'm not reporting total failure. I've merely cut the field in half. I shall go doggedly forward. Beyond the Bronx lies New Rochelle."

"Who lives there?"

"Rachel Hager. Third on my list. And then there's Pagan Kelly, a Bennington chick whom you can find in almost any picket line whose protest is silly."

"Two suspects," Ellery said. "But don't rush into it. Go off somewhere and ponder your attack."

"You mean you want me to dawdle?"

"Isn't that what you do best? But not in my apartment. I've got to get this story finished."

"Did you finish the journal?" the playboy asked, not stirring.

"I'm busy with my own mystery."

"Have you gone far enough to spot the killer?"

"Brother," Ellery said, "I haven't spotted the murderer in my own story yet."

"Then I'll leave you to your labors. Oh. Suppose we never will find out who sent you the manuscript?"

"I think I'd manage to survive."

"Where did you get your reputation?" the young man asked nastily. He left.

Ellery's brain dangled, like a foot that has fallen asleep. The typewriter keys looked a thousand yards away. Vagrant thoughts began to creep into the vacuum. How was dad getting along in Bermuda? What were the

99

latest sales figures on his last book? He did not have to ask himself who had sent the manuscript by way of Grant Ames III. He already knew the answer to that. So, by a natural process, he began to wonder about the identity of Sherlock Holmes's visitor from Paris (he had peeked ahead).

After a short battle, which he lost, he went into the bedroom. He plucked Dr. Watson's journal from the floor, where he had left it, and stretched out on his bed to read on.

CHAPTER VIII

A VISITOR FROM PARIS

THE ENSUING DAYS were most trying. In all our association, I had never seen Holmes so restless, and so difficult to get along with.

After our interview with Lord Carfax, Holmes ceased to communicate with me. My overtures were ignored. It then occurred to me that I had intruded further into this case than into any of the investigations I had shared with him. In the light of the chaos I had managed to create, my chastisement seemed just. So I retreated into my customary rôle of bystander, and awaited developments.

They were slow in coming. Holmes had turned, like the Ripper, into a creature of the night. He vanished from Baker Street each evening, to return at dawn and spend the day in brooding silence. I kept to my own room, knowing that solitude was essential to him at such times. His violin wailed at intervals. When I could stand its scratching no longer, I took myself off into the welcome hubbub of London's streets.

On the third morning, however, I was appalled at his appearance.

"Holmes! In God's name!" I cried. "What has happened to you?"

There was an ugly purple contusion below his right temple. The sleeve of his jacket had been ripped away, and a gashed wrist had no doubt bled copiously. He walked with a limp, and he was as begrimed as any of the street Arabs he so often sent on mysterious missions.

"A dispute in a dark by-way, Watson."

"Let me attend to those wounds!"

I snatched my satchel from my room and returned. Grimly he displayed the bloody knuckles of his right fist. "I attempted to lure our enemy into the open, Watson. I succeeded." Pressing Holmes into a chair, I begin my examination. "I succeeded, but I failed."

"You take perilous risks."

"The assassins, two of them, rose to my bait."

"The same ones who attacked us?"

"Yes. My purpose was to lay one of them by the heels, but my revolver jammed—of all the accursed luck! —and both got away."

"Pray relax, Holmes. Lie back. Close your eyes. Perhaps I should give you a sedative."

He made an impatient gesture. "These scratches are nothing. It is my failure that pains me. So near and yet so far. Had I been able to hold one of those scoundrels, I should have got the name of his employer soon enough, I warrant you."

"Is it your feeling that these brutes are perpetrating the butcheries?"

"Good heavens, no! They are wholesome, healthy bruisers beside the depraved creature we seek." Holmes stirred nervously. "Another, Watson, a bloodthirsty tiger loose in the jungle of London."

The dread name came into my head. "Professor Moriarty?"

"Moriarty is not involved in this. I have checked his activities, and his whereabouts. He is occupied elsewhere. No, it is not the Professor. I am certain our man is one of four."

"To which four do you refer?"

Holmes shrugged his shoulders. "What does it matter so long as I am unable to put my hands upon him?"

The physical strain had begun to wear on him. Holmes lay back in the chair and gazed, heavy-lidded, at the ceiling. But the fatigue did not extend to his mental faculties.

"This 'tiger' you refer to," said I. "What does it profit him to go about killing luckless prostitutes?"

"The affair is far more tangled than that, Watson. There are several dark threads that twist and turn in this maze."

"That repulsive simpleton at the hostel," I muttered.

Holmes's smile was humourless. "I fear, my dear Watson, that you have your finger upon the wrong thread."

"I cannot believe that Michael Osbourne is in no way involved!"

"Involved, yes. But—"

He did not finish, because at that moment the bell sounded below. Mrs. Hudson was soon opening the door. Holmes said, "I have been expecting a visitor; he is prompt. Pray remain, Watson. My jacket, if you please. I must not look like a street-brawler who has dropped in for medical treatment."

By the time he had got into the garment and lighted his pipe, Mrs. Hudson was ushering a tall, blond, good-looking chap into our parlour. I estimated him to be in his mid-thirties. He was assuredly a man of good breeding; except for a single startled glance, he made no reference to Holmes's battered appearance.

"Ah," said Holmes. "Mr. Timothy Wentworth, I believe. You are welcome, sir. Take the seat by the fire. The air is damp and chill this morning. This is my friend and colleague, Dr. Watson."

Mr. Timothy Wentworth bowed acknowledgement, and took the proffered chair. "Your name is famous, sir," said he, "as is that of Dr. Watson. I am honoured to make your acquaintance. But I have a busy schedule in Paris, and I tore myself away only because of my regard for a

103

friend, Michael Osbourne. I have been utterly mystified by his unheralded disappearance from Paris. If I can do anything to help Michael, I shall consider the Channel crossing well worth the inconvenience."

"A most admirable loyalty," said Holmes. "Perhaps we can enlighten each other, Mr. Wentworth. If you will tell us what you know about Michael's sojourn in Paris, I shall pick up for you the end of his story."

"Very well. I met Michael some two years ago, when we enrolled together at the Sorbonne. I think I was attracted to him because we were opposites. I am myself somewhat retiring; indeed, my friends consider me shy. On the other hand, Michael was possessed of a fiery spirit, sometimes gay, sometimes bordering upon the violent, when he felt that he had been put upon. He never left the least doubt as to his opinion on any subject; however, by making allowances for each other's short-comings, we got on well together. Michael was very good for me."

"And you for him, sir, I've no doubt," said Holmes. "But, tell me. What did you learn of his personal life?"

"We were candid with each other. I quickly learned that he was second son to a British nobleman."

"Was he embittered by the misfortune of second birth?"

Mr. Timothy Wentworth frowned as he considered his answer. "I should have to say yes, and yet no. Michael had a tendency to break out, one might say, to go wild. His breeding and background forbade such behaviour, and caused a guilt to arise within him. He needed to palliate that guilt, and his position as second son was something against which to revolt, and thus justify his wildness." Our young guest stopped self-consciously. "I'm putting it badly, I fear."

"To the contrary," Holmes assured him, "you express yourself with admirable clarity. And I may assume, may

I not, that Michael harboured no bitterness against either his father or his elder brother?"

"I am sure he did not. But I can also understand the contrary opinion of the Duke of Shires. I see the Duke as a man of proud, even haughty, spirit, preoccupied with the honour of his name."

"You see him exactly as he is. But pray go on."

"Well, then there came Michael's alliance with that woman." Timothy Wentworth's distaste was apparent in his tone. "Michael met her in some Pigalle rat's-nest. He told me about her the following day. I thought nothing of it, considering it a mere alliance. But now I see Michael's withdrawal from our friendship as dating from that time. It was slow when measured in hours and days, but swift enough as I look back upon it—from the time he told me of the meeting, to the morning he packed his clothes in our digs, and told me that he had married the woman."

I interjected a comment. "You must have been shocked, sir."

"Shocked is hardly the term. I was stunned. When I found words with which to remonstrate, he snarled at me to mind my own affairs, and left." Here, a deep regret appeared in the young man's honest, blue eyes. "It was the termination of our friendship."

"You did not see him again?" murmured Holmes.

"I tried, and did see him briefly on two other occasions. Word of that sort of thing, of course, cannot be kept secret—a short time later, Michael was dropped from the Sorbonne. When I heard this, I made a point of seeking him out. I found him living in an unspeakable sty on the Left Bank. He was alone, but I presume his wife was living there with him. He was half-drunk, and received me with hostility—a different man by far from the one I had known. I could not even begin to reach him, so I placed some money upon the table and left. A fortnight later, I met him in the street, near the Sorbonne. His appearance cut me to the quick. It was as if a lost soul had returned to gaze wistfully upon the opportunities he had thrown away. His defiance remained, however. When I attempted to accost him, he snarled at me and slunk away."

"I gather, then, that you have never laid eyes upon his wife?"

"No, but there were rumours concerning her. It was whispered about that the woman had a confederate, a man with whom she had consorted both before and after her marriage. I have no certain knowledge of that, however." He paused, as though pondering the tragic fate of his friend. Then he raised his head and spoke with more spirit. "I believe that Michael was somehow put upon in that disastrous marriage, that in no way did he deliberately seek to bring shame upon his illustrious name."

"And I believe," said Holmes, "that I can reassure you on that point. Michael's kit of surgical instruments has recently come into my possession, and I discovered upon examining it that he had carefully covered the emblazoned coat of arms it bore with a piece of velvet cloth."

Timothy Wentworth's eyes widened. "He was forced to dispose of his instruments?"

"The point I wish to make," continued Holmes, "is that this very act of concealing the insignia indicates, not only shame, but an effort to protect the name he has been accused of seeking to disgrace."

"It is intolerable that his father will not believe that. But now, sir, I have told you all I know, and I am eager to hear what you have to tell me."

Holmes was markedly reluctant to reply. He arose from his chair and took a quick turn across the room. Then he stopped. "There is nothing you can do for Michael, sir," said he.

Wentworth seemed ready to spring up. "But we made a bargain!"

"Michael, some time after you last saw him, suffered an accident. At present he is little more than mindless flesh, Mr. Wentworth. He remembers nothing of his past, and his memory will probably never return. But he is being well cared-for. As I have said, there is nothing you can do for him, and in suggesting that you do not see him I am attempting to spare you further distress."

Timothy Wentworth turned his frown upon the floor, considering Holmes's advice. I was glad when he sighed, and said, "Very well, Mr. Holmes, then it is over." Wentworth came to his feet and extended his hand. "But if there is anything I can ever do, sir, please get in touch with me."

"You may depend upon it."

After the young man left, Holmes stood in silence, gazing from the window at our departing visitor. When he spoke, it was in so low a voice that I could scarcely catch his words. "The more grievous our faults, Watson, the closer a true friend clings."

"What was that, Holmes?"

"A passing thought."

"Well, I must say that young Wentworth's account changes my opinion of Michael Osbourne."

Holmes returned to the fire to stab a restless poker at the log. "But I am sure you realise that his hearsay was of far more significance than his fact."

"I confess I do not follow you."

"The rumour that the woman, Michael's wife, had a male accomplice throws additional light upon the problem. Now, who could this man be, Watson, other than our elusive missing link? Our tiger who set assassins upon us?"

"But how did he know?"

"Ah, yes. How did he discover that I was on his trail before I knew it myself? I think we shall make another call upon the Duke of Shires, at his town-house in Berkeley Square."

We were not destined, however, to make that visit. At that moment the bell again rang downstairs, and we heard Mrs. Hudson again answer the door. A great clatter followed; the caller had rushed past our landlady and was taking the stairs two at a time. Our door burst open, and there he stood, a thin and pimple-faced youth with a great air of defiance about him. His manner was such that my hand moved automatically towards a fire-iron.

"W'ich o' you gents is Mr. Sherlock 'Olmes?"

"I, my lad," answered Holmes; and the youth extended a parcel wrapped in brown paper. "This 'ere's to be given to yer, then."

Holmes took the parcel and opened it with no ceremony.

"The missing scalpel!" cried I.

Holmes had no chance to reply. The messenger had bolted, and Holmes whirled about. "Wait!" he shouted. "I must speak with you! You shall not be harmed!"

But the boy was gone. Holmes rushed from the room. I hastened to the window, and beheld the youth fleeing down the street as though all the devils of Hell were after him, Sherlock Holmes swiftly in his wake.

Ellery's Legman Legs It Again

"RACHEL?"

She looked back over her shoulder. "Grant! Grant Ames!"

"Just thought I'd drop in," said the playboy.

"So sweet of you!"

Rachel Hager wore a pair of blue jeans and a tight sweater. She had long legs and a slim body, but there were plenty of curves. Her mouth was full and wide, and her eyes were an odd off-brown, and her nose was pugged. She looked like a madonna who had run into a door.

This pleasing paradox did not escape Grant Ames III. She didn't look like this the other day, he thought, and pointed to what she had been doing in the backyard.

"I didn't know you grew roses."

Her laugh revealed the most beautiful buck teeth. "I try. Heavens, how I try. But my thumb stays its natural color. What brings you into the wilds of New Rochelle?" She slipped off her gloves and lifted a strand of hair off her forehead. The shade was mouse brown, but Grant was sure that, bottled, it would have lined them up at the cosmetic counters.

"Just driving by. Hardly got a chance to say hello at Lita's the other day."

"I was there by accident. I couldn't stay around."

"I noticed you didn't swim."

"Why, Grant! Such a nice compliment. Most girls are

noticed when they do. How about the patio? I'll bring you a drink. Scotch, isn't it?"

"At times, but at the moment I could do with a frosty iced tea."

"Really? I'll be right back."

When she returned, Grant watched her cross her long legs in a lawn chair too low to be comfortable. For some reason he was stirred. "Lovely garden."

That enchanting buck-toothed laugh again. "You should see it after the kids leave."

"The kids?"

"From the orphanage. We bring a group over once a week, and it's *wild*. They do respect the roses, though. One little girl just sits and stares. Yesterday I gave her an ice-cream cone and it melted all over her hand. It was that Mammoth Tropicana over there. She tried to kiss it."

"I didn't know you worked with children." As a matter of cold fact, Grant had not had the least idea what Rachel did, and until now had not cared a whit.

"I'm sure I get more out of it than they do. I'm working on my Master's now, and I have time to spare. I was thinking of the Peace Corps. But there's so much to do right here in the U.S.—in town, in fact."

"You're gorgeous," Grant unbelievingly heard himself mutter.

The girl looked up quickly, not sure she had heard him right. "What on earth are you talking about?"

"I was trying to remember how many times I've seen you. The first was at Snow Mountain, wasn't it?"

"I think it was."

"Jilly Hart introduced us."

"I remember because I broke my ankle that trip. But how can *you* possibly remember? With your harem?"

"I'm not entirely irresponsible," said Grant stuffily.

"I mean, why should you? Me? You've never shown—"

"Would you do me a favor, Rachel?"

"What?" asked Rachel suspiciously.

"Go back and do what you were doing when I got here. Dig at your roses. I want to sit here and look at you."

"Is this your latest line?"

"It's very strange," he mumbled.

"Grant. What did you come here for?"

"What?"

"I said, what did you come here for?"

"Damned if I can remember."

"I'll bet you can," the girl said, a little grimly. "Try."

"Let me see. Oh! To ask if you'd put a brown manila envelope on the seat of my Jag at Lita's. But the hell with that. What kind of fertilizer do you use?"

Rachel squatted. Grant had visions of *Vogue.* "I have no formula. I just keep mixing. Grant, what's the matter with you?"

He looked down at the lovely brown hand on his arm. *My God! It's happened!*

"If I come back at seven, will you have a frock on?" he asked.

She looked at him with a dawning light. "Of course, Grant," she said softly.

"And you won't mind my showing you off here and there?"

The hand squeezed. "You darling."

"Ellery, I've found her, I've found her!" Grant Ames III babbled over the telephone.

"Found whom?"

"THE Woman!"

"Who put the envelope in your car?" Ellery said in a peculiar voice.

"Who put what?" said Grant.

"The envelope. The journal."

"Oh." There was a silence. "You know what, Ellery?"

"No. What?"

"I didn't find out."

Ellery went back to Dr. Watson, shrugging.

CHAPTER IX

THE LAIR OF THE RIPPER

I COULD DO nothing but wait. Infected by Holmes's fever of impatience, trying to occupy the hours, I assessed the situation, endeavouring to apply the methods I had so long witnessed Holmes employ.

His identification of the Ripper as one of four men came in for its share of my ponderings, you may be sure, but I was confused by other elements of the puzzle—Mycroft's assertion that, as yet, his brother did not have all the pieces, and Holmes's yearning to come to grips with the "tiger" prowling London's by-ways. If the Ripper was one of four persons whom Holmes had already met, where did the "tiger" fit in? And why was it necessary to locate him before the Ripper could be brought to book?

Elation would have been mine, had I known that at that moment I myself held the key. But I was blind to both the key and its significance; and, when this knowledge did come to me, it brought only humiliation.

Thus I fretted away the hours with but a single break in the monotony. This occurred when a note was delivered to Baker Street by a smartly-uniformed page-boy. "Sir, a message from Mr. Mycroft Holmes to Mr. Sherlock Holmes."

"Mr. Holmes is absent at the moment," said I. "You may leave the note."

After I had dismissed the page, I examined the note. It was in a sealed envelope, from the Foreign Office. The Foreign Office was where Mycroft had his being.

My fingers were itching to tear the flap, but of course I did not. I pocketed the missive and went on with my pacing. The hours passed, with no sign of Holmes. At times, I went to the window and watched the fog that was settling in over London. As twilight fell, I remarked to myself what a fortuitous night this would be for the Ripper.

This had evidently occurred to the maniac also. Quite dramatically, upon the heels of my thought, there came a message from Holmes, delivered by an urchin. I tore it open with trembling fingers as the boy waited.

> *My dear Watson:*
> *You will give this boy a half-crown for his trouble, and meet me post-haste at the Montague Street morgue.*
>
> *Sherlock Holmes*

The urchin, a bright-faced lad, had never before received such a handsome *pourboire*, I am certain. In my relief, I gave him a crown.

In no time at all I was in a hansom, urging the cabman on through the thickening pea-soup that be-fogged the streets. Fortunately, the Jehu had the instincts of a homing-pigeon. In a remarkably short time he said, "The right-'and door, guv'ner. Walk strite on and watch yer nose, or yer'll bang into the ruddy gite."

I found the gate with some groping, went in, and through the court, and found Holmes by the raised table in the mortuary.

"Still another, Watson," was his portentous greeting.

Dr. Murray and the imbecile were also present. Murray stood silently by the table, but Michael-Pierre cringed by the wall, naked fear upon his face.

As Murray remained motionless, Holmes frowned.

Said he, sharply, "Dr. Murray, you do not question Dr. Watson's stomach for it?"

"No, no," replied Murray, and drew back the sheet.

But my stomach was tested, nonetheless. It was the most incredible job of butchery on a human body that the sane mind could conceive. With demented skill the Ripper had gone berserk. In decency, I refrain from setting down the details, save for my gasp, "The missing breast, Holmes!"

"This time," responded Holmes, grimly, "our madman took away a trophy."

I could endure it no longer; I stepped down from the platform. Holmes followed. "In God's name, Holmes," cried I, "the beast must be stopped!"

"You are in good company with that prayer, Watson."

"Has Scotland Yard been of any aid to you?"

"Rather, Watson," replied he, sombrely, "have I been of any aid to Scotland Yard? Very little, I fear."

We took our leave of Murray and the imbecile. In the swirling fog of the street, I shuddered. "That wreck who was once Michael Osbourne...Is it my fancy, Holmes, or did he crouch there for all the world like Murray's faithful hound, expecting a kick for some transgression?"

"Or," replied Holmes, "like a faithful hound sensing his master's horror and seeking to share it. You are obsessed with Michael Osbourne, Watson."

"Perhaps I am." I forced my mind to turn back. "Holmes, were you able to apprehend the messenger who took to his heels?"

"I clung to his trail for several blocks, but he knew London's labyrinths as well as I. I lost him."

"And you spent the rest of the day how, may I ask?"

"A portion of it in the Bow Street Library, attempting to devise a pattern from a hypothetical projection of the madman's brain."

He began walking slowly through the fog-bank, I by his side. "Where are we going, Holmes?"

"To a particular section of Whitechapel. I laid out the pattern, Watson, a positioning of all the known Ripper murders, super-imposed upon a map of the area which they cover. I spent several hours studying it. I am convinced that the Ripper works from a central location, a room, or a flat, a sanctuary from which he ventures forth and to which he returns."

"You propose to search?"

"Yes. We shall see if shoe-leather will reward us where arm-chair has failed."

"In this fog it will take leg-work indeed."

"True, but we have certain advantages on our side. For example, I have made it a point to question the witnesses."

This startled me. "Holmes! I did not know there were any."

"Of a sort, Watson, of a sort. On several occasions, the Ripper has worked perilously close to detection. In fact, I suspect that he deliberately arranges his murders in that fashion, out of contempt and bravado. You will recall our brush with him."

"Well do I!"

"At any rate, I have decided, from the sounds of his retreating footsteps, that he moves from the perimeter of a circle toward its centre. It is within the centre of that circle that we shall search."

Thus we plunged, that fog-choked night, towards the cesspools of Whitechapel into which the human sewage from the great city drained. Holmes moved with a sure-footedness that bespoke his familiarity with those malodorous depths. We were silent, save when Holmes paused to inquire, "By the way, Watson, I trust you thought to drop a revolver into your pocket."

"It was the last thing I did before I left to join you."

"I, too, am armed."

We ventured first into what proved to be an opium-den. Struggling for breath in the foul fumes, I followed as Holmes moved down the line of bunks, where the addicted victims lay wrapped in their happy dreams. Holmes paused here and there for a closer inspection. To some he spoke a word; at times, he received a word in return. When we left, he appeared to have garnered nothing of value.

From there we invaded a series of low public-houses, where we were greeted for the most part by sullen silence. Here, also, Holmes spoke *sotto voce* with certain of the individuals we came upon, in such a manner that I was sure he was acquainted with some of them. On occasion, a coin or two passed from his hands into a filthy palm. But always we moved on.

We had left the third dive, more evil than the others, when I could contain myself no longer.

"Holmes, the Ripper is not a cause. He is a result."

"A result, Watson?"

"Of such corrupt places as these."

Holmes shrugged his shoulders.

"Does it not stir you to indignation?"

"I would of course welcome a sweeping change, Watson. Perchance in some future, enlightened time, it will come about. In the meanwhile, I am a realist. Utopia is a luxury upon which I have no time to dream."

Before I could reply, he pushed open another door, and we found ourselves in a brothel. The reek of cheap scent almost staggered me. The room into which we entered was a parlour, with half a dozen partially-naked females seated about in lewd poses as they awaited whoever might emerge from the fog.

Quite candidly, I kept shifting my eyes from the inviting smiles and lascivious gestures that greeted us on all sides. Holmes rose to the occasion with his usual equanimity.

Giving his attention to one of the girls, a pale, pretty little thing who sat clad in nothing but a carelessly open robe, he said, "Good-evening, Jenny."

"Evenin', Mr. 'Olmes."

"That address I gave you, of the doctor. Did you visit him?"

"That I did, sir. 'E gave me a clean bill o' 'ealth, 'e did."

A beaded curtain parted and a fat *madame* with eyes like raisins stood regarding us. "What brings you out on a night like this, Mr. Holmes?"

"I am sure you know, Leona."

Her face turned sulky. "Why do you think my girls are off the streets? I don't want to lose any of them!"

A plump, over-painted creature spoke angrily. "H'it's a bloody shyme, h'it is—a poor gel gettin' pushed by bobbies all the time."

Another commented, "Better than a bloody blade in yer gut, dearie."

"Almost 'ad me a gent, h'I did, wot lives at the Pacquin. 'E was a'goin' up the stairs, all w'ite tie an' cape, 'e was, an 'e stops w'en 'e sees me. Then this bobby shoves 'is dish outa the fog. ' 'Ere now, dearie,' said 'e. 'Off to yer crib. This is no night to be about.' " The girl spat viciously upon the floor.

Holmes's voice was even as he said, "The gentleman fled, I presume?"

"Up t' 'is room, w'ere else? But not a-takin' me with 'im!"

"An odd place for a gentleman to live, would you not say?"

The girl wiped her mouth with the back of her hand. " 'E can live we'er 'e pleases, blarst 'is eyes!"

Holmes was already moving towards the door. As he passed me, he whispered, "Come, Watson. Hurry, hurry!"

Back in the fog, he gripped my hand and pulled me

recklessly forward. "We have him, Watson! I'm certain of it! Visits—questions—a dropped comment—and we come upon the trail of a fiend who can do many things. But making himself invisible is not one of them!"

Sheer exultancy rang from every word as Holmes dragged me after him. A few moments later I found myself stumbling up a flight of narrow stairs against a wooden wall.

The exertion of the chase had taxed even Holmes's superb stamina; and, as we climbed, he gasped out his words. "This Pacquin is a sordid rooming-house, Watson. Whitechapel abounds with them. Fortunately, I was familiar with the name."

I glanced upwards, and saw that we were approaching a partly-open door. We reached the top of the stairs, and Holmes hurled himself inside. I staggered after him.

"What accursed luck!" cried he. "Someone has been here before us!"

Not in all our days together had I seen Holmes present such an image of bitter frustration. He loomed in the middle of a small, shabbily-furnished room, revolver in hand, grey eyes a-blaze.

"If this was the lair of the Ripper," cried I, "he has fled."

"And for good, no doubt of that!"

"Perhaps Lestrade was on his trail."

"I wager not! Lestrade is off bumbling through some alley."

The room had been well-torn up in the Ripper's haste to get away. As I sought words to ease Holmes's disappointment, he grimly took my arm. "If you doubt that the maniac operates from this den, Watson, look there."

I followed his pointing finger, and saw it. The grisly trophy—the breast missing from the corpse in the Montague Street morgue.

I have seen violence and death enough, but this was

worse. There was no heat here, no anger; only dank horror, and my stomach revolted against it.

"I must leave, Holmes. I shall wait for you below."

"There is no point in my remaining, either. What is to be seen here is to be seen quickly. Our quarry is far too cunning to leave the slightest clue behind."

At that moment, possibly because my mind sought a diversion, I remembered the message. "By the way, Holmes, a messenger brought a note to Baker Street this afternoon from your brother Mycroft. In the excitement, I forgot." I handed him the envelope forthwith, and he tore it open.

If I expected his thanks, I was disappointed. After reading the missive, Holmes raised cold eyes. "Would you care to hear what Mycroft writes?"

"Indeed I would."

"The note reads: 'Dear Sherlock: A bit of information has come to me, in a way I shall explain later, which will be of value to you. A man named Max Klein is the proprietor of a Whitechapel sink named The Angel and Crown. Klein, however, purchased the place only recently; some four months ago, in fact. Your brother, Mycroft.'"

I was too confounded to suspect which way the wind lay. I give myself that grace, at least, because so much more can be explained only by admitting to an abysmal stupidity. At any rate, I blurted forth, "Oh, yes, Holmes. I was aware of that. I got the information from the girl with whom I talked during my visit to The Angel and Crown."

"Did you indeed?" asked Holmes, dangerously.

"A redoubtable fellow, this Klein. It occurred to me that it had not taken him long to impress his personality upon the place."

Holmes exploded, raising his fists. "Great God in Heaven! I wade knee-deep in idiots!"

The wind I had not suspected struck me with its blast. My mouth dropped open. I managed feebly to say, "Holmes, I do not understand."

"Then there is no hope for you, Watson! First, you garner the exact information that would have enabled me to solve this case, and you blithely keep it to yourself. Then, you forget to give me the note containing that same vital fact. Watson! Watson! Whose side are you on?"

If I had been confused before, I was now completely at sea. No protest was possible; and defiance, defence of my self-esteem, was out of the question.

But Holmes was never a man to belabour a point. "The Angel and Crown, Watson!" cried he, leaping towards the door. "No, to the morgue first! We shall present that devil with a sample of his own handiwork!"

Ellery Hears From The Past

THE DOORBELL rang.

Ellery slammed down the journal. It was undoubtedly that alcoholic blotter again. He debated answering, glanced guiltily at his typewriter, and went out into the foyer and opened the door.

It was not Grant Ames, but a Western Union messenger. Ellery scribbled his name and read the unsigned telegram.

WILL YOU FOR BLANK'S SAKE PLUG IN YOUR TELEPHONE QUESTION MARK AM GOING STIR CRAZY EXCLAMATION POINT

"No answer," Ellery said. He tipped the messenger and went straightway to obey the Inspector's order.

Muttering to himself, he also plugged in his shaver and plowed its snarling head through his beard. As long as he keeps phoning, he thought, he's still in Bermuda. If I can browbeat him into just one more week ...

The revitalized phone rang. Ellery snapped the shaver off and answered. Good old dad.

But it was not good old dad. It was the quavering voice of an old lady. A very old lady.

"Mr. Queen?"

"Yes?"

"I have been expecting to hear from you."

"I must apologise," Ellery said. "I planned to call on

you, but Dr. Watson's manuscript caught me at a most awkward time. I'm up to my ears in a manuscript of my own."

"I'm so sorry."

"I'm the one who's sorry, believe me."

"Then you have not had the time to read it?"

"On the contrary, it was a temptation I couldn't resist, deadline or not. I've had to ration myself, though. I still have three chapters to go."

"Perhaps, Mr. Queen, with your time so limited, I'd best wait until you have completed your own work."

"No—please. My problems there are solved. And I've looked forward to this chat."

The cultured old voice chuckled. "I needn't mention that my advance order for your new mystery has been placed, as always. Or would you consider that deliberate flattery? I hope not!"

"You're very kind."

There was something under the quiet, precise diction, the restraint, the discipline, something Ellery felt sure of, possibly because he had been expecting it—a tension, as if the old lady were almost to the snapping point.

"Were you at all troubled as to the authenticity of the manuscript, Mr. Queen?"

"At first, frankly, when Grant brought me the manuscript, I thought it a forgery. I soon changed my mind."

"You must have thought my mode of delivery eccentric."

"Not after reading the opening chapter," Ellery said. "I understood completely."

The old voice trembled. "Mr. Queen, *he did not do it. He was not the Ripper!*"

Ellery tried to soothe her distress. "It's been so many years. Does it really matter any longer?"

"It does, it does! Injustice always matters. Time changes many things, but not that."

Ellery reminded her that he had not yet finished the manuscript.

"But you know, I feel that you know."

"I'm aware in which direction the finger's pointing."

"And keeps pointing, to the end. But it is not true, Mr. Queen! Sherlock Holmes was wrong for once. Dr. Watson was not to blame. He merely recorded the case as it unfolded—as Mr. Holmes dictated. But Mr. Holmes failed, and did a great injustice."

"But the manuscript was never published—"

"That makes no genuine difference, Mr. Queen. The verdict was known, the stain indelibly imprinted."

"But what can I do? No one can change yesterday."

"The manuscript is all I have, sir! The manuscript and that abominable lie! Sherlock Holmes was not infallible. Who is? God reserves infallibility for Himself alone. The truth must be hidden in the manuscript somewhere, Mr. Queen. I am pleading with you to find it."

"I'll do my best."

"Thank you, young man. Thank you so very much."

With the connection safely broken, Ellery slammed down the phone and glared at it. It was a miserable invention. He was a nice guy who did good works and was kind to his father, and now this.

He was inclined to wish a pox on the head of John Watson, M.D., and all adoring Boswells (where was his?); but then he sighed, remembering the old lady's trembling voice, and sat down with Watson's manuscript again.

CHAPTER X

THE TIGER OF THE ANGEL
AND CROWN

"I EARNESTLY HOPE, my dear fellow, that you will accept my apology."

These words from Holmes were the most welcome I had ever received. We were back in the street, pushing along through the fog, as there were no hansoms cruising Whitechapel that night.

"You were totally justified, Holmes."

"To the contrary. I displayed a childish petulance that ill becomes a grown man. Blaming others for one's own mistakes is indefensible. The information, which you so readily extracted from the girl Polly, I should have had the intelligence to come by long ago. You actually proved an ability to do my work far better than I have done it myself."

All of which was specious; but Holmes's praise salved my pride, nonetheless.

"I cannot accept the accolade, Holmes," I protested. "It did not occur to me that Klein was indicated as your missing link."

"That," said Holmes, still over-generous, "was because you neglected to turn your perceptions in the proper direction. We were looking for a strong man, a man brutal and remorseless. Klein, from what you told me, filled that bill; also, from what I myself observed in the pub. Others in Whitechapel would qualify as equally vicious, although

125

it is true that the other bit of information points directly to Klein."

"His recent purchase of the pub? When you explain, it becomes quite simple."

"What happened is now predictable, with only the smallest percentage in favour of error. Klein saw an opportunity in the person of Michael Osbourne. Both Michael and, beyond all doubt, the prostitute Angela, of whom Michael became enamoured, were weak individuals, easily controlled by this cruelly dominating man. It was Klein who engineered the infamous marriage that ruined Michael Osbourne."

"But to what purpose?"

"Blackmail, Watson! The plan failed when Michael stood upon his better nature and refused his cooperation. The plot was saved by Klein only through sheer luck, I am certain. Thus he was able to extort enough money to buy The Angel and Crown, and has no doubt feathered his noisome nest since."

"But so much is still unanswered, Holmes. Michael —reduced to a state of imbecility. His wife Angela— whom, I remind you, we have yet to locate—hideously scarred."

"In good time, Watson, in good time."

My confusion was the more compounded by Holmes's tone of confidence.

"Their present plight, you may be sure, is the result of Klein's rage at being thwarted by Michael's refusal to be a party to the blackmail scheme. No doubt it was Klein who administered that brutal beating to Michael which brought about his imbecility. How Angela became disfigured is not so evident, but I suggest that she went to Michael's defence."

At this moment, we walked out of the fog into a pocket of visibility, and saw the gate to the mortuary.

I shuddered. "And now, Holmes, you plan to transport the body of that poor girl to The Angel and Crown?"

"Hardly, Watson," said he, absently.

"But you mentioned confronting Klein with his handiwork."

"That we shall do, I promise you."

Shaking my head, I followed Holmes through the mortuary into the hostel, where we found Dr. Murray ministering to the blackened eye of a man who had probably imbibed violence with his pint in some pub.

"Is Michael Osbourne on the premises?" demanded Holmes.

Dr. Murray was haggard. Over-work, and the thankless task of caring for the uncared-for, were taking their toll. Said he, "A short time ago, I would not have recognised that name—"

"Please," interrupted Holmes. "Time is paramount, Dr. Murray. I must take him away with us."

"To-night? Now?"

"There have been certain developments, Doctor. Before dawn, the Ripper will have been run to earth. The account must be settled with the beast responsible for Whitechapel's blood-bath."

Dr. Murray was as bewildered as I. "I do not understand. Do you mean, sir, that the Ripper is a creature of an even greater villain?"

"In a sense. Have you seen Inspector Lestrade lately?"

"He was here an hour ago. He is undoubtedly out in the fog somewhere."

"Tell him, should he return, to follow me to The Angel and Crown."

"But why are you taking Michael Osbourne with you?"

"To confront his wife," said Holmes, impatiently. "Where is he, man? We waste precious time!"

"You will find him in the small room off this end of the mortuary. That is where he sleeps."

We found the imbecile there, and Holmes shook him gently awake. "Angela is waiting for you," said he.

There was no flicker of understanding in the vacant eyes; but, with the trust of a child, he accompanied us into the fog. It was now so thick that we depended completely upon Holmes's hound-like senses to keep us on our course. And, so sinister was the atmosphere of London that night, I half-expected to feel the bite of a blade between my ribs at any moment.

But my curiosity was strong. I ventured a query. "Holmes, I assume that you expect to find Angela Osbourne at The Angel and Crown."

"I am certain of it."

"But what purpose is served by facing her with Michael?"

"The woman may be reluctant to speak. There will be a certain shock-value in suddenly confronting her with her husband."

"I see," said I, although I did not, quite; and lapsed back into silence.

At last there was the sound of a hand tapping upon wood, and I heard Holmes say, "This is it, Watson. Now we search."

A faintly glowing window indicated that it was a domicile of some sort. Said I, "Was that the front door you tapped upon?"

"It was, but we must find another. I wish to reach the upper rooms unseen."

We pawed along the wall and around a corner. Then a breeze stirred the fog, thinning it.

Holmes had thought to borrow a dark lantern during

our visit to the hostel, although he had not used it during our journey. It might well have brought us to the unwelcome attention of foot-pads. It now served us in good stead, outlining a rear door, apparently used for the delivery of beer-kegs and spirits. Holmes pushed the panel open and reached inside. "The hasp has been recently broken," said he; and we went through stealthily.

We were in a store-room. I could hear the muffled noise from the public-room, but it appeared that our presence had gone undetected. Holmes quickly found a laddered ascent to the upper storey. We climbed it with caution, crept through a trap-door, and found ourselves at the end of a dimly-lit corridor.

"Wait here with Michael," whispered Holmes. He soon returned. "Come!"

We followed him to a closed door; a line of light shone upon our boot-tips. Holmes pressed us back against the wall and tapped upon the panel. There was quick movement inside. The door opened, and a female voice queried, "Tommy?"

Holmes's hand was in like a snake and locked over a shadowed face. "Do not scream, Madam," said he, in a commanding whisper. "We mean you no harm. But we must speak to you."

Holmes warily relaxed the pressure of his hand. The woman's voice asked, "Who are you?" in understandable fear.

"I am Sherlock Holmes. I have brought your husband."

I heard a gasp. "You have brought Michael—here? In God's name, why?"

"It was the prudent thing to do."

Holmes entered the room and nodded to me to follow. Grasping Michael's arm, I did so.

Two oil-lamps were burning, and in their light I saw a

E—SHJR

woman, wearing a veil whose gauzy texture did not quite conceal a hideous scar. It was undoubtedly Angela Osbourne.

At the sight of the imbecile—her husband—she grasped the arms of the chair in which she sat, and half-arose. But then she sank back with the rigidity of a corpse, her hands gripped together.

"He does not recognise me," she murmured in despair.

Michael Osbourne stood silently by me, regarding her with his empty eyes.

"As well you know, Madam," said Holmes. "But the time is short. You must speak. We know that Klein is responsible for both your husband's condition and your disfigurement. Tell me about the interlude in Paris."

The woman wrung her hands. "I will not waste time making excuses for myself, sir. There are none. As you can perhaps see, I am not like those poor girls downstairs who fell into their shameful calling through poverty and ignorance. I am what I have become because of that beast, Max Klein.

"You wish to know about Paris. I went there because Max had arranged an assignation for me with a wealthy French merchant. Whilst this was taking place, I met Michael Osbourne, and he was taken with me. Believe me, sir, I had no intention of shaming him; but when Max Klein arrived in Paris, he saw an opportunity to use the smitten youth for his own ends. Our marriage was the first step in his plan, and he compelled me to use my wiles. Michael and I were married, despite my tearful protestations to Max.

"Then, with Michael safely in his clutch, Max sprang his trap. It was the most blatant blackmail, Mr. Holmes. He would acquaint the Duke of Shires with the facts, said he, and threaten to reveal his son's wife for what I was, parading me before all the world, unless his Grace paid."

"But this never came about," said Holmes, eyes gleaming.

"No. Michael had more spine than Max had anticipated. He threatened to kill Max, even made the attempt. It was a dreadful scene! Michael stood no chance before Max's brute strength. He felled Michael with a blow. But then Max's temper, his sheer savagery of nature, seized him, and he administered the terrible beating that resulted in Michael's present condition. Indeed, the beating would have ended in Michael's death, had I not intervened. Whereupon Max plucked a knife from the table, and rendered me as you see me. His rage left him in the nick of time, averting a double murder."

"His beating of Michael and mutilation of you did not make him abandon his plan?"

"No, Mr. Holmes. Had it done so, I am sure Max would have left us in Paris. Instead, using the considerable sum of money he took from Michael, he brought us back to Whitechapel and purchased this public-house."

"The money was not gained through blackmail, then?"

"No. The Duke of Shires was generous with Michael until he disowned him. Max stripped Michael of every penny he had. Then he imprisoned us here, in The Angel and Crown, plotting, no doubt, to go on with whatever infamous plan he had in mind."

"You said he brought you *back* to Whitechapel, Mrs. Osbourne," said Holmes. "Is this Klein's habitat?"

"Oh, yes, he was born here. He knows its every street and alley. He is greatly feared in this district. There are few who dare cross him."

"What was his plan? Do you know?"

"Blackmail, I am sure. But something happened to balk him; I never discovered what it was. Then Max came to

131

me one morning, fiercely elated. He said that his fortune was made, that he needed Michael no longer, and planned to murder him. I pleaded with him. Perhaps I was able to touch off a spark of humanity in his heart; in any case, he humoured me, as he put it, and delivered Michael to Dr. Murray's hostel, knowing his memory was gone."

"The good fortune that elated Klein, Mrs. Osbourne. What was its nature?"

"I never learned. I did ask him if the Duke of Shires had agreed to pay him a large sum of money. He slapped me and told me to mind my affairs."

"Since that time you have been a prisoner in this place?"

"A willing one, Mr. Holmes. Max has forbidden me to leave this room, it is true, but my mutilated face is my true gaoler." The woman bowed her veiled head. "That is all I can tell you, sir."

"Not quite, Madam!"

"What else?" said she, head rising.

"There is the matter of the surgeon's-case. Also, of an unsigned note informing Lord Carfax of his brother Michael's whereabouts."

"I have no idea, sir—" she began.

"Pray do not evade me, Madam. I must know everything."

"There seems to be no way of keeping a secret from you!" cried Angela Osbourne. "What are you, man or devil? If Max were to get wind of this, he would surely kill me!"

"We are your friends, Madam. He will not hear it from us. How did you discover that the case had been pledged with Joseph Beck?"

"I have a friend. He comes here at the risk of his life to talk to me and do my errands."

"No doubt the 'Tommy' you expected when I knocked upon your door?"

"Please do not involve him, Mr. Holmes, I beg of you!"

"I see no reason to involve him. But I wish to know more about him."

"Tommy helps out at times at the Montague Street Hostel."

"You sent him there originally?"

"Yes, for news of Michael. After Max delivered him to the hostel, I slipped out one night, at great risk to myself, and posted the note you refer to. I felt I owed Michael at least that. I was sure Max would never find out, because I could see no way in which Lord Carfax might trace us, with Michael's memory gone."

"And the surgeon's-case?"

"Tommy overheard Sally Young discuss with Dr. Murray the possibility of pawning it. It occurred to me that it might be a means of interesting you to turn your talents, Mr. Holmes, to the apprehension of Jack the Ripper. Again I slipped out, redeemed the case, and posted it to you."

"Removing the post-mortem scalpel was deliberate?"

"Yes. I was sure you would understand. Then when I heard no word of your entrance into the case, I became desperate, and I sent the missing scalpel to you."

Holmes leaned forward, his hawk's-face keen. *"Madam, when did you decide that Max Klein is the Ripper?"*

Angela Osbourne put her hands to her veil, and moaned. "Oh, I don't know, I don't know!"

"What made you decide he was the monster?" asked Holmes, inexorably.

"The nature of the crimes! I can conceive of no one save Max as being capable of such atrocities. His maniacal temper. His dreadful rages . . .

We were not destined to hear any more from Angela Osbourne. The door burst open, and Max Klein sprang into the room. His face was contorted by an unholy

133

passion that he was just able, it appeared, to hold in leash. He had a cocked pistol in his hand.

"If either of you moves so much as a finger," cried he, "I'll blow you both to Hell!"

There could be little doubt that he meant it.

Ellery's Legman's Last Bow

THE DOORBELL rang.
Ellery ignored it.
It rang again.
He kept on reading.
A third time.
He finished the chapter.
When he finally got there, his caller had given up and left. But he had slipped a telegram under the foyer door.

BOSOM FRIEND DASH WHILE HUNTING A
THORN YOUR LEGMAN FOUND A ROSE STOP
HE WILL HUNT NO MORE STOP HER NAME IS
RACHEL HAGER BUT A NAME CANNOT DO
JUSTICE TO HER STOP SHE WENT TO THAT
PARTY ONLY BECAUSE I WAS THERE COMMA
A FACT THAT POPS MY BUTTONS STOP LAW-
FUL WEDLOCK IS NEXT STOP STOP WE PLAN
CHILDREN STOP OUR JOINT LOVE TO YOU
STOP

GRANT

"Thank God I'm shed of *him*," said Ellery, aloud and went back to Sherlock Holmes.

CHAPTER XI

HOLOCAUST

I THINK THAT Holmes would have braved Klein's pistol, were it not that the proprietor of The Angel and Crown was immediately followed into Mrs. Osbourne's room by a man whom I recognised as one of the thugs who had attacked Holmes and me. Under the muzzles of two weapons, Holmes perforce held himself in check.

Max Klein's rage became evil satisfaction.

"Tie them up," snarled he, to his confederate. "And the man who tries to resist gets a bullet through his head."

The thug tore the cords from the curtains and swiftly lashed Holmes's hands behind his back, whilst I stood helplessly by. He thereupon treated me in like manner, going even further under Klein's command.

"Shove our good doctor into that chair and lash his ankles to its legs." Why Klein should have considered me a greater threat than Holmes, I did not understand. What courage I possess is thoroughly tempered, I fear, with a great desire to live out the years allotted me by the Almighty.

As his creature did his bidding, Klein turned to Holmes. "Did you think you could walk into my place undetected, Mr. Holmes?"

Replied Holmes, quietly, "I am curious to know how our entrance was discovered."

Klein laughed, a brutal sound. "One of my men had to roll some empty kegs out. Not spectacular, I grant you, Mr. Holmes. But I've got you just the same."

"Getting me, as you phrase it," said Holmes, "and keeping me, Klein, may be a steed of a different colour."

It was evident to me that Holmes was attempting to gain time. But it was to no avail. Klein surveyed my bonds, found them to his liking, and said, "You will come with me, Mr. Holmes. I shall deal with you in private. And if you expect help from below, you will be disappointed. I have cleared the place; it is closed and locked."

The thug indicated Angela Osbourne with a worried glance. "Is it safe leavin' this cull with 'er? She might loose 'im."

"She would not dare," Klein laughed again. "Not if she knows what's good for her. She still values her miserable life."

This proved depressingly true. After Holmes and Michael Osbourne were dragged away, Angela Osbourne was impervious to all persuasion. I spoke with as urgent eloquence as I could command, but she only stared at me in despair, moaning, "Oh, I dare not, I dare not."

Thus passed several of the longest minutes of my life, as I struggled against my bonds, telling myself that Holmes would yet save the day.

Then came the most dreadful moment of all.

The door opened.

The chair in which I sat trussed was so situated that, when I heard the panel swing inwards, I was unable to see who stood there. Angela Osbourne, however, sat in view of the doorway. I could only look in her direction for a clue.

She arose from her chair. Somehow the veil slipped aside, and I saw that hideously-scarred face clearly. Every fibre of my being shrank at the unspeakable mutilation which Klein had visited upon her; but it was made even more repulsive by the wild expression with which she regarded the intruder in the doorway. Then she spoke.

E*

"The Ripper! Oh, God in Heaven! It is Jack the Ripper!"

I confess with shame that my first reaction was relief. The man advanced within my sight, and when I beheld the slim, aristocratic figure, clad in top-hat, perfectly-fitting evening clothes, and opera cape, I cried thankfully, "Lord Carfax! You have come providentially!"

The ghastly truth dawned upon me an instant later, when I espied the glittering knife in his hand. He glanced my way, but only for a moment, and with no sign of recognition. And I beheld the madness in that noble face, a hungry, wild-beast's urge to destroy.

Angela Osbourne was incapable of further outcry. She sat in frozen terror as the lordly Ripper rushed upon her and in a trice tore away her upper clothing. She could only mumble a prayer before Lord Carfax plunged the weapon into her uncovered breast. His clumsy efforts at dissection are best not described; suffice it to say that they did not approach the skill of his earlier mutilations, undoubtedly because he felt pressed for time.

As the body of Angela Osbourne fell to the floor in a welter of blood, the madman seized upon one of the oil-lamps and extinguished the flame. Unscrewing the wick-holder, he proceeded to pour out the oil. His intent was all too clear. Around the room he dashed, like some demon out of Hell, leaving oil in his wake; and then out into the corridor, from whence he returned soon with an empty lamp, which he flung to the floor in a shower of glass.

And then he seized the other lamp, and with it ignited the pool of oil at his feet.

Strangely, he did not flee; even at that worst moment of my life, I wondered why. As it developed, his maniacal ego proved my salvation and his destruction. As the flames mounted, following the river of oil into the corridor, he rushed at me. I closed my eyes and consigned my soul to its

Maker. To my stupefaction, instead of slaying me, he slashed my bonds.

With dilated eyes, he hauled me upright and dragged me through the flames towards the nearest window. I sought to struggle with him, but with his maniac's strength he threw me savagely against the window, and the glass shattered.

It was then that he uttered the cry that has echoed through my nightmares ever since.

"Carry the message, Dr. Watson!" he screamed. "Tell them that Lord Carfax is Jack the Ripper!"

With that, he thrust me through the window. Flames had caught my clothing; and I remember that, ludicrously, I slapped at them as I fell the one storey to the street. Then there was a stunning impact with the stones below, I thought I heard running footsteps, and unconsciousness mercifully gripped me.

I knew no more.

CHAPTER XII

THE END OF JACK THE RIPPER

THE FIRST FACE I beheld was that of Rudyard, the friend who had taken over my practice as locum tenens. I was in my room at Baker Street.

"A near thing, Watson," said he, as he felt my pulse.

Awareness came flooding back to me. "How long have I slept, Rudyard?"

"Some twelve hours. I gave you a sedative when they carried you here."

"My condition?"

"A most salutary one, under the circumstances. A broken ankle; a sprained wrist; burns no doubt painful, but superficial."

"Holmes. Where is he? Has he been—?"

Rudyard gestured. There was Holmes, seated grave-faced, at the opposite side of my bed. He was pale, but appeared otherwise unharmed. Thankfulness welled up in me.

"Well, I must be off," said Rudyard. To Holmes he said, "See that he doesn't talk too long, Mr. Holmes."

Rudyard departed, saying that he would be back to dress my burns, and warning me again not to tax my strength. But, even through my pain and discomfort, I could not restrain my curiosity. Holmes, I fear, was in no better case, despite his concern for my condition. So I soon found myself relating what had occurred in poor Angela Osbourne's room after Klein had forced him from it.

Holmes nodded, but I could see that he was struggling with a decision. Finally, he said to me, "I fear, old friend, that we have gone through our last adventure together."

"Why do you say that?" asked I, overwhelmed with dismay.

"Because your good wife will never again entrust your welfare to my bungling hands."

"Holmes!" cried I. "I am not a child!"

He shook his head. "You must go back to sleep."

"You know that cannot be until you tell me how you managed to escape from Klein. In a dream, after my sedation, I saw your mangled remains..."

I shuddered, and he placed his hand upon mine in a rare display of affection. "My opportunity arose when the staircase burst into flames," said Holmes. "Klein had glutted himself with gloating over me, and he was just raising his weapon when the flames swept down. He and his henchman died in the fire as the structure went up like tinder. The Angel and Crown is now a roofless ruin."

"But you, Holmes! How—?"

Holmes smiled, and shrugged his shoulders. "There was never a doubt but that I could slip my bonds," said he. "You know my dexterity. All that lacked was the chance, and the fire provided it. Unhappily, I was unable to save Michael Osbourne. He seemed to welcome death, poor fellow, and resisted my efforts to drag him out; indeed, he threw himself into the flames, and I was compelled to abandon his body to save my life."

"A blessing in disguise," I muttered. "And that infamous beast, Jack the Ripper?"

Holmes's grey eyes were clouded with sadness; his thoughts appeared to be elsewhere. "Lord Carfax died also. And also from choice, I am certain, like his brother."

"Naturally. He preferred death by fiery immolation to the hangman's noose."

Holmes seemed elsewhere still. In the gravest of voices, he murmured, "Watson, let us respect the decision of an honourable man."

"Honourable man! Surely you are jesting? Oh, I see. You refer to his lucid moments. And the Duke of Shires?"

Holmes's chin was sunken upon his chest. "I am a bearer of dire news about the Duke, too. He has taken his life."

"I see. He could not bear the awful revelation of his first son's crimes. How did you learn this, Holmes?"

"I proceeded directly from the fire to his Berkeley Square residence. Lestrade accompanied me. We were too late. He had already had the news of Lord Carfax. Whereupon he had fallen upon the sword he kept concealed in his stick."

"A true nobleman's death!"

I fancied Holmes nodded; it was the merest inclination of his head. He seemed deeply depressed.

"An unsatisfactory case, Watson, most unsatisfactory," said he. And he fell silent.

I sensed his wish to conclude the conversation, but I would not have it so. I had forgotten all about my broken ankle and the pain of my burns.

"I do not see why, Holmes. The Ripper is dead."

"Yes," said he. "Really, Watson, you must rest now." He made as if to rise.

"I cannot rest," said I, artfully, "until all the pieces are in place." He sank back with resignation. "Even I am able to follow the sequence of those last events that lead up to the fire. The maniacal Ripper, functioning from behind his philanthropic *façade* as Lord Carfax, did not know the identity or the whereabouts of Angela Osbourne or Max Klein. Am I correct?"

Holmes did not reply.

"When you found his lair," I pressed on, "I am sure you knew also who he was?"

Here Holmes nodded.

"Then we went to the hostel, and although we did not see him there, he saw us and heard us—that, or he came shortly thereafter and learned of The Angel and Crown from Dr. Murray, who would have had no reason to withhold the information. Lord Carfax followed us and discovered the beer-keg entrance, as we did."

"Lord Carfax preceded us," said Holmes, abruptly. "You will recall that we found the hasp recently broken."

"Amended. He must have been able to move through the foggy streets more surely than we. No doubt we interrupted his stalking of Angela Osbourne, who was slated to be his next victim. He must have been lying in wait in a corridor-doorway whilst we entered Mrs. Osbourne's room."

Holmes did not contest this.

"Then, realising you had run him to earth, he determined to conclude his infamous career in the blaze of mad defiance that his monstrous ego dictated. His final words to me were, 'Carry the message, Dr. Watson! Tell them that Lord Carfax is Jack the Ripper!' Only an egomaniac would have said that."

Holmes came to his feet with finality. "At any rate, Watson, Jack the Ripper will prowl no more. And now we have defied your doctor's orders long enough. I insist that you sleep."

With that, he left me.

Ellery Visits The Past

ELLERY PUT the Watson manuscript down thoughtfully. He barely heard the click of the lock and the opening and closing of the front door.

He looked up to find his father standing in the study doorway.

"Dad!"

"Hi, son," said the Inspector with a defiant grin. "I just couldn't stand it down there any more. So here I am."

"Welcome home."

"Then you're not sore?"

"You stayed longer than I expected."

The Inspector came in, scaled his hat to the sofa, and turned to regard his son with relief. It soon became concern.

"You look like hell. What's wrong, Ellery?"

Ellery did not reply.

"How do I look?" asked his father cunningly.

"A damsite better than when I packed you off."

"You're sure *you're* all right?"

"I'm fine."

"Don't give me that. Is your story going sour?"

"No, it's going fine. Everything's fine."

But the old man was not satisfied. He sat down on the sofa and crossed his legs and said, "Tell me all about it."

Ellery shrugged. "I should never have been born the son of a cop. All right, something's happened. An interlocking of events, past and present. The loosening of an old knot."

"Talk English."

"Grant Ames dropped in on me."

"You told me that."

"I got sucked into the manuscript. One thing led to another. And here I am."

"I don't get it."

Ellery sighed. "I suppose I'll have to tell you all about it." And he talked for a long time.

"And that's how it stands, dad. She believes absolutely in his innocence. She's nursed it all her life. I suppose she didn't know what to do about it until, in her old age, she suddenly got this inspiration to drag me into it. Inspiration!"

"What are you going to do?"

"I'd just made up my mind to pay her a visit when you walked in on me."

"I should think so!" Inspector Queen got up and took the journal from Ellery's hand. "The way I see it, son, you've got absolutely no choice. After all, she's asked for it."

Ellery got to his feet. "Why don't you read the manuscript while I'm gone?"

"That's just what I'm going to do."

He drove north into Westchester, taking Route 22 until he came to Somers. He passed the wooden elephant at the main intersection, a reminder that Barnum & Bailey's Circus had one wintered there. In Putnam County he thought of the Revolutionary heroes, hoping they were all in a hero's heaven somewhere.

But these were surface thoughts. In depth he was thinking of the old lady he would find at the end of his journey. They were not pleasant thoughts.

He finally turned in at a trim little cottage with a doll's-house drive, got out, and reluctantly went up to the front door. It opened to his knock immediately, as if she had been lying in wait for him. He had half wished she would not be at home.

"Deborah Osbourne Spain," he said, looking down at her. "Hello."

She was very old, of course; she must be in her late 80s, according to his calculations. The manuscript had not given her age on the day Holmes and Watson visited Shires Castle, except in approximate figures. She could be 90.

Like so many very old ladies, especially the tiny plumpish ones, there was a slightly withered-apple look to her, with the bloom still touching her cheeks. Her bosom was large for her size, and fallen, as if tired of its weight. Only her eyes were young. They were bright, and direct, and they twinkled in spite of themselves.

"Do come in, Mr. Queen."

"Could you make it Ellery, Mrs. Spain?"

"It is something I have never quite become accustomed to," she said, ushering him into a cozy little parlor, as mid-Victorian as Victoria's bustle, Ellery thought. It was like stepping into 19th Century England. "I mean, the American habit of instant familiarity. However—take that Morris chair, Ellery—if you wish."

"I wish." He sat down and looked about. "I see you've kept the faith."

She seated herself in a ducal chair, in which she looked lost. "What else does an ancient Englishwoman have?" she asked with a faint smile. "I know—I sound disgustingly Anglophilic. But it's so difficult to get away from one's beginnings. Actually, I'm quite comfortable here. And a visit to New Rochelle once in a while to see Rachel's roses rounds out my existence."

"Rachel *was* the one."

"Oh, yes. At my request."

"Miss Hager is related to you how, exactly?"

"My granddaughter. Shall we have tea?"

"Not just now, if you don't mind, Mrs. Spain," said Ellery. "I'm too chockful of questions. But first." He sat on the edge of the chair, avoiding the lace anti-macassar. "You saw him. You met them both. Holmes. Watson. How I envy you!"

Deborah Osbourne Spain's eyes looked far into the past. "It was so very long ago. But of course I remember them. Mr. Holmes's glance, sharp as a sword. And so reserved. When I put my hand in his, I'm sure it disconcerted him. But he was very sweet. They were both such gentlemen. That above all. In those days, Ellery, being a gentlemen was important. Of course, I was a little girl, and I recall them as giants, towering to the sky. As I suppose they were, in a way."

"May I ask how you came by the manuscript?"

"After Dr. Watson wrote it, the journal was turned over by Mr. Holmes to the Osbourne estate. It became the responsibility of the estate's solicitor, bless him! He was so faithful to my interests. Then, after I was grown, and shortly before he died, he told me about the manuscript. I begged for it, and he sent it to me. His name was Dobbs, Alfred Dobbs. I think of him so often."

"Why did you wait so long, Mrs. Spain, before doing what you did?"

"Please. Everyone calls me Grandma Deborah. Won't you?"

"Grandma Deborah it shall be."

"I don't know why I waited so long," the old lady said. "The idea of asking an expert to verify my conviction never crystallized in my mind, although I am sure it has been there for a long time. Lately, a feeling that there is a need to hurry has come over me. How much longer can I live? And I should like to die in peace."

The implicit plea moved Ellery to her aid. "Your decision to send me the manuscript came from the manuscript itself, I take it?"

"Yes. Afterwards, Mr. Ames confided in Rachel about the hunt you sent him on."

"Grant's searching accomplished an end, though not the one I expected," Ellery smiled.

"Bless him! Bless them both. I knew he gave you no help, Ellery. I also knew you would find me, just as Mr. Holmes had no difficulty in tracing the owner of the surgeon's kit. But I'm still curious as to how you did it."

"It was elementary, Grandma Deborah. It was obvious from the first that the sender had some personal interest in the case. So I put a call through to a friend of mine, a genealogist. He had no trouble tracing you from Shires Castle, as a child, to the custody of the San Francisco branch of the family. I had the names of Grant's four young ladies, and I was sure one of the names would pop up somewhere. From your marriage to Barney Spain in 1906 my expert got to the marriage of your daughter. And, lo and behold, the man your daughter married was named Hager. Q.E.D." His smile became a look of concern. "You're tired. We can put this off for another time."

"Oh, no! I'm fine." The young eyes pleaded. "He was a wonderful man, my father. Kind, gentle. He was not a monster. He was not!"

"You're sure you don't want to lie down?"

"No, no. Not until you've told me..."

"Then lie back in your chair, Grandma. Relax. And I'll talk."

Ellery took the withered old hand in his, and he talked against the ticking of the grandfather clock in the corner, its pendulum, like a mechanical finger, wiping the seconds off the face of time.

The little frail hand in Ellery's squeezed at irregular

148

intervals. Then it stopped squeezing, and lay in Ellery's hand like an autumn leaf.

After a while, there was a movement of the portieres at the archway to the parlor, and a middle-aged woman appeared, wearing a white housedress.

"She's fallen asleep," Ellery whispered.

He carefully laid the old hand on her breast and tip-toed from the room.

The woman accompanied him to the door. "I'm Susan Bates. I take care of her. She falls asleep like that more and more."

Ellery nodded and left the cottage and got into his car and drove back to Manhattan, feeling very tired himself. Even old.

The Ripper Case Journal
Final Note
January 12, 1908

HOLMES VEXES ME. I confess, because he was out of England for an extended period, that I took it upon myself, against his wish, to put my notes for the Jack the Ripper case into narrative form. Twenty years have now passed. For nine of these, a new heir, a distant relation, has borne the Shires title. One, I might add, who spends but a fraction of his time in England, and cares little for either the title or its illustrious history.

I had come to feel, however, that it was high time the world was informed of the truth about the Ripper case, which held an equally illustrious place—if that is the word!—in the history of crime, and about Holmes's struggle to end the monster's bloody reign in Whitechapel.

On Holmes's return from abroad, I broached this to him, expressing myself in the most persuasive terms I could muster. But he is adamant in his refusal.

"No, no, Watson, let the bones lie mouldering. The world would be no richer from the publication of the story."

"But Holmes! All this work—"

"I am sorry, Watson. But this is my last word in the matter."

"Then," said I, with ill-concealed annoyance, "allow me to present you with the manuscript. Perhaps you will find use for the paper as pipe-lighters."

"I am honoured, Watson, and touched," said he, most

cheerfully. "In return, allow me to present you with the details of a little matter I have just brought to a successful conclusion. You may apply to it your undeniable *flair* for melodrama, and submit it to your publishers without delay. It has to do with a South American sailing-man, who came very close to duping a European financial syndicate with a 'genuine' roc's-egg. Perhaps *The Case of the Peruvian Sinbad* will in some measure assuage your disappointment."

And thus, matters now stand.

Ellery Explains

ELLERY'S ARRIVAL was timely. Inspector Queen had just finished reading Dr. Watson's Ripper manuscript, and he was staring at the journal with marked dissatisfaction. He turned his stare on Ellery.

"Just as well it wasn't published. Holmes was right."

"I thought so, too." Ellery went to the bar. "Damn Grant! I forgot to order scotch."

"How did it turn out?"

"Better than I expected."

"Then you lied like a gentleman. Good for you."

"I didn't lie."

"What?"

"I didn't lie. I told her the truth."

"Then," said Inspector Queen coldly, "you're a ratfink. Deborah Osbourne loved and believed in her father. She also believes in you. Your mind is certainly crooked enough to have twisted the truth a little."

"I didn't have to twist the truth."

"Why not? Tell me that! A little old lady—"

"Because, dad," said Ellery, sinking into his swivel chair, "Lord Carfax wasn't Jack the Ripper. A lie wasn't necessary. Deborah's father was no monster. She was right about him all along. She knew it, I knew it—"

"But—"

"And so did Sherlock Holmes."

There was a silence of great length while *pater* tried to catch up with *filius* and failed.

"But it's all down here, Ellery!" protested the Inspector.

"Yes, it is."

"Richard Osbourne, this Lord Carfax, caught with the knife in his hand, butchering his last victim—why, Watson was an eyewitness!—wrote it all down!"

"Your point is, I take it, that Watson was an able reporter?"

"I'd say so. He also knew the evidence of his own eyes!"

Ellery got up and went over to his father, picked up the journal, and returned to his chair. "Watson was also human. He was oversubjective. He saw what Holmes wanted him to see. He reported what Holmes told him."

"Are you saying that Holmes was pulling a fast one?"

"You're damned right I am. The devious thing is that in this case every word from his lips was gospel. It's what he didn't say that counts."

"All *right*. What was it that he didn't say?"

"He didn't at any time, for instance, call Jack the Ripper by the name of Richard Osbourne or Lord Carfax."

"You're quibbling," snorted the Inspector.

Ellery riffled through the old journal. "Dad, didn't you spot the inconsistencies in the case? Certainly you weren't satisfied with the blackmail bit?"

"The blackmail? Let me see..."

"It went like this. Max Klein saw an opportunity for blackmail by conniving a marriage between Michael Osbourne and Angela, a prostitute. Considering the Duke of Shires' pride of name, that made sense from Klein's viewpoint. But it didn't work. The marriage became public knowledge."

"But Klein admitted to Angela that the plan had failed."

"Not exactly. He told her, after he'd brought the couple back to London, that the marriage was no longer important as a basis for blackmail. He'd found a better

153

gimmick. Klein lost all interest in Michael and Angela after he discovered this new weapon, obviously a better one than the marriage."

"But the manuscript never said—"

"Dad, who was Klein? What was he? Holmes was aware from the start of his importance, even before the man was identified—when he was Holmes's missing link. And when Holmes confronted Angela, he pried a vital piece of information out of her. To quote her on the subject of Klein: 'Oh, yes, he was born here. He knows its every street and alley. He is greatly feared in this district. There are few who would dare cross him.'"

"So?"

"So what was the great secret Klein had discovered?"

"*The identity of Jack the Ripper,*" said the Inspector slowly. "A man like that, who had an intimate knowledge of Whitechapel and its people—"

"Of course, dad. That's what it had to be. And with the knowledge of the Ripper's identity Klein got rich blackmailing—"

"Lord Carfax."

"No. You'll recall that Lord Carfax was trying desperately to locate Klein and Angela. Blackmailers confront their victims."

"Maybe Carfax knew all the time."

"Then why didn't he strike earlier? Because he only learned that night at the morgue that Klein and Angela were at The Angel and Crown!"

"But Carfax struck at Angela, not Klein."

"Further proof that he was not the blackmail victim. He mistakenly saw his brother's wife as the evil force in the Osbourne disaster. That's why he killed her."

"But none of that is enough to base—"

"Then let's find some more. Let's follow Holmes and Watson that last night. You already know what *appeared* to happen. Let's see what really did. In the first place, there were two men on the trail of the Ripper that night— Sherlock Holmes *and* Lord Carfax. I'm sure Carfax already had his suspicions."

"What indication is there that Carfax was on the Ripper's trail?"

"I'm glad you asked that question," Ellery said sententiously. "Acting on the tip he'd picked up in Madame Leona's whorehouse, Holmes set out on the last leg of his search. He and Watson arrived at the room in the Pacquin—"

"And Holmes said, 'If this was the lair of the Ripper, he has fled.'"

"Holmes didn't say that, Watson did. Holmes cried, 'Someone has been here before us!' There's a world of difference in the two statements. One was the observation of a romantic. The other, Holmes's, of a man trained to read a scene with photographic accuracy."

"You have a point," the older Queen admitted.

"A vital one. But there are others."

"That both Holmes and Lord Carfax found the lair of Jack the Ripper at practically the same time?"

"Also that Carfax saw Holmes and Watson arrive at the Pacquin. He waited outside and followed them to the morgue. It had to be that way."

"Why?"

"In order for Carfax to act as he did, he needed two items of information—the identity of the Ripper, which he got at the Pacquin, and the place where he could find Angela and Klein, which he overheard at the morgue."

Inspector Queen got up and retrieved the journal. He searched and read: "'And that infamous beast, Jack the Ripper?' Watson asked Holmes that question. Holmes answered, 'Lord Carfax died also—'"

"Hold it," Ellery said. "None of this out-of-context business. Give me all of it."

"Quote: 'Holmes's grey eyes were clouded with sadness; his thoughts appeared to be elsewhere. "Lord Carfax died also. And also from choice, I am certain, like his brother."'"

"That's better. Now tell me, would Sherlock Holmes be sad over the death of Jack the Ripper?"

Inspector Queen shook his head and read on. "'Naturally. He no doubt preferred death by fiery immolation to the hangman's noose.'"

"Watson's words, not Holmes's. What Holmes then said was, 'Let us respect the decision of an honourable man.'"

"To which Watson replied, 'Honourable man! Surely you are jesting? Oh, I see. You refer to his lucid moments. And the Duke of Shires?'"

"Watson drew an unwarranted inference from what Holmes had said. Let's quote Holmes again: 'I proceeded directly from the fire to his'—meaning the Duke's—'Berkeley Square residence . . . He had already had the news of Lord Carfax. Whereupon he had fallen upon the sword he kept concealed in his stick.'"

"And Watson exclaimed, 'A true nobleman's death!'"

"Again Watson was fooled by his own preconceptions and his misunderstanding of Holmes's deliberate indirection. Look, dad. When Holmes reached the Duke of Shires's townhouse, he found the Duke dead. But 'he (the Duke) had already had the news of Lord Carfax.' I ask you how could the Duke have 'already had the news of Lord Carfax'? The implication is clear that the Duke had been at his Pacquin lair, where Lord Carfax confronted him, after which he went home and killed himself."

"Because the Duke was the Ripper! And his son, knowing it, took the blame on himself to save his father's reputation!"

156

"Now you've got it," said Ellery gently. "Remember again what Carfax said to Watson—to spread the word that *he* was Jack the Ripper. He wanted to make dead sure that the guilt fell on his shoulders, not his father's."

"Then Holmes was right," murmured Inspector Queen. "He didn't want to give Lord Carfax's sacrifice away."

"And Deborah's faith in her father has been vindicated after three-quarters of a century."

"I'll be damned!"

Ellery took Dr. Watson's journal from his father's hand and opened it to the "Final Note."

"*'The Case of the Peruvian Sinbad,'*" he muttered. "Something about a roc's egg..." His eyes glinted. "Dad, do you suppose Holmes could have been pulling Watson's leg about that one, too?"

-EQ-